# Math for ELLs

# Math for ELLs

*As Easy as Uno, Dos, Tres*

Jim Ewing

ROWMAN & LITTLEFIELD
Lanham • Boulder • New York • London

Published by Rowman & Littlefield
A wholly owned subsidiary of The Rowman & Littlefield Publishing Group, Inc.
4501 Forbes Boulevard, Suite 200, Lanham, Maryland 20706
www.rowman.com

Unit A, Whitacre Mews, 26-34 Stannary Street, London SE11 4AB

British Library Cataloguing in Publication Information Available

**Library of Congress Cataloging-in-Publication Data**

Library of Congress Control Number:2019954120

978-1-4758-5307-0 (cloth : alk. paper)
978-1-4758-5308-7 (paper : alk. paper)
978-1-4758-5309-4 (electronic)

∞™ The paper used in this publication meets the minimum requirements of American
National Standard for Information Sciences—Permanence of Paper for Printed Library
Materials, ANSI/NISO Z39.48-1992.

# Contents

## Textboxes in the Book

## Figures in the Book

## Tables in the Book

**Activities in the Appendices**

~

# Foreword

Mathematics teachers are generally committed to providing access to rigorous and cognitively demanding mathematics to all of their students. With the increase in many classrooms of English language learners (ELLs, now better referred to as emergent bilinguals), teachers seek high-quality resources that are effective in providing access for them too.

*Math for ELLs: As Easy as Uno, Dos, Tres* is such a resource. It incorporates a large number of research-based best practices and includes other practices that enhance the learning of ELLs. For example, practices designed specifically for Spanish-speaking ELLs are provided.

Author Jim Ewing writes from his experiences as a classroom teacher of ELLs and as a researcher concentrating on ELLs, preservice teacher education, mathematics education, and students in poverty. He also brings his passion for and commitment to ELLs becoming proficient in mathematics. Dr. Ewing views ELLs from a whole student approach, addressing both the cognitive and affective aspects and behaviors of learning mathematics.

Dr. Ewing emphasizes working with individuals by interacting with them and "knowing" who they are. He reiterates several times that some ideas work for some students and other ideas work for other students and that it is critical for teachers to acknowledge these differences by knowing who their students are and appreciating the cultural capital and assets they bring to the classroom. We are reminded that ELLs are learning mathematics and acquiring language, including the academic language of the discipline, concurrently.

The book incorporates both productive and receptive language enhancements for ELLs. Too often ELLs are given mostly receptive language assignments and aren't provided classroom experiences in productive language. Dr. Ewing stresses the need to maintain high cognitive demand of the mathematics, and he provides the rationale for why this is important.

This book is exemplary in promoting the whole child approach from the beginning in the introduction to the final chapter of "Putting It All Together." Each chapter builds on the previous and each is important in the teaching of ELLs. Read the whole book. This is a high-quality resource that is effective in providing access to the mathematics that leads to proficiency for ELLs.

What is most exciting about this book is that once teachers read and use the whole book, they will be empowered to incorporate their own ideas and expertise to design their own practices that can meet the needs of ELLs.

Susie W. Håkansson
Past President and Member Services Chair
TODOS: Mathematics for ALL

~

# Preface

I was an elementary teacher for twenty-five years and made many mistakes, especially toward ELLs. I used to believe that math was universal and didn't require language. In Spain I worked at an international private elementary school with English as the language of instruction. We required new students to take a test before they were admitted.

One summer the principal was away, so she asked me to administer a math test for a nine-year-old Russian girl who spoke very little English. After all, math is math, right? Despite not knowing English, I expected her to be able to answer the math questions, which were mostly arithmetic. When I went to check on the girl, she had only answered a few questions.

I talked with the parents and told them how their daughter had fared. The parents were in disbelief and asked me to call the girl in. She was in tears and managed to explain in Russian to her parents that she did not understand what she had to do. The parents asked me what some symbols meant and then translated for their daughter. Even though the girl was under pressure, with the help of her parents she did math sums mentally that were even challenging for me.

The assessment was designed to measure the student's mathematical ability, but because the symbols are different in Russia, she didn't understand them. Later in the year, the girl's teacher had to give her extra challenging problems—the math problems that the rest of the students were doing were too easy for her. I had almost made a serious error by assuming that the student was not strong in math, but the truth was, she merely lacked access (chapter 2).

Since making this mistake with the Russian student, I have dedicated years of study and research on how we might best meet the needs of English language learners (ELLs) in math. The purpose of this book is to share these strategies with other teachers. About three-quarters of the ELLs in the United States speak Spanish. While recognizing the importance of meeting the needs of each student in math, this book focuses on offering teachers strategies specifically to meet the needs of Spanish-speaking ELLs.

It makes sense for me to write about Spanish-speaking ELLs because my experiences and research for the past thirty-five years have dealt with helping teachers work with Spanish speakers. I am fluent in Spanish, and when I was an administrator in Spain I would help English-speaking teachers understand how to teach math to their Spanish-speaking students.

Moreover, as a professor working in Texas, my teaching, service, and research have a strong focus on meeting the needs of Spanish-speaking ELLs in math. Most of the strategies that I suggest in this book are research based. My dissertation and seven articles I have written are mostly about how we might teach math to Spanish-speaking ELLs.

The strategies that I suggest in this book also come from my university teaching experiences. As part of my mathematics education course, my preservice teachers go to a local school and tutor math to fourth graders; many of these students are Spanish-speaking ELLs. Most of the elementary preservice teachers in my class have had negative math experiences and enter my class with negative math mindsets.

Before we can engage students to have positive math mindsets and engage in productive struggle (chapter 4), we should also experience having a positive math mindset and engaging in productive struggle ourselves. Boosting relationships, being positive, taking risks, and persevering are other tools for engaging Spanish-speaking ELLs that are discussed in this book.

Of course the strategies discussed in this book are only suggestions. Please do not assume that these strategies work for all Spanish-speaking ELLs. There is no substitute for getting to know your students and their preferences. When I was twelve years old I lived in Wales for a year, and my friends asked me if all Americans had TVs in our bathrooms. It happens that I was an American who grew up without a TV in my house. Likewise, each of your students will be unique. However, I share with you what I have learned in thirty-five years working with Spanish-speaking ELLs.

I hope you will enjoy the book and, more importantly, I hope you will join me in my passion for improving how we teach math to Spanish-speaking ELLs.

~

# Acknowledgments

I dedicate this book to my parents—I could not have written this book without them. I thank them for their support throughout this process. They have helped with the editing and given helpful advice for the past four years.

I would like to thank Eric Jensen. Four years ago I observed Eric give a workshop, and he has been my mentor ever since. He not only encouraged me to write this book but has also taught me how to give motivating workshops to teachers.

I would also like to give thanks to the following educators: LeAnn Nickelsen, Shauna King, Bryan Harris, Eric Larison, Tracie Steel, Jenny Severson, David Rische, Brandon Fox, Deborah Williams, Adam Akerson, Susan Ferguson, Daya Hill, Tim Mullican, Nancy White, Lola Moore, Lindsey Turner, Julia Wells, Evelyn Sauceda, Gabriele Keese, Michelle Foreman, Danielle Johnson, Rhonda McCallie, Jane Tarr, John Lamb, Deborah Plowman, Dusty Jones, Mark Montgomery, Frank Kros, Amy Kines, Glenda Hinsley, Michelle Nance, Jodie Weddle, and Susan Håkansson. And thank you to all the students I have taught in the past thirty-four years.

~

# Introduction

Most teachers plan their instruction for the non-ELLs. Then they try to adapt what they teach to include ELLs. This book reverses that approach. It focuses on how to meet the needs of *Spanish-speaking ELLs* first, and then, if you want, you can try to adapt these strategies to meet the needs of other ELLs or non-ELLs.

There are many definitions for ELLs. The definition used in this book refers to those students who speak a language other than English at home (Lucas, 2011). Therefore this book is written for teaching students who speak Spanish at home even if they do not receive English as a second language (ESL) services at school. Cultural strategies for teaching math are also offered that may be helpful to Latinx (this term is gender-neutral or gender-fluid and includes both Latinas and Latinos) students, whether or not they speak fluent Spanish.

## English Language Learners (ELLs) vs. Emergent Bilinguals (EBs)

One way we can start meeting the needs of ELLs is by changing the way we refer to them. Please pretend that you are in a teacher workshop and draw a picture in the air with your left hand. (If you are left-handed you probably already know how it feels to be in a right-handed world.) How did that feel? Perhaps it was fun because it was exploratory. But what would happen if you were told that you could no longer use your right hand? From now on, you have to draw with your opposite hand, and you are given the label of "left-handed learner" or an "LHL."

Imagine how you would feel if you were singled out and left in the classroom to learn how to draw with your left hand and nobody paid attention to how you drew with your right hand. How would you feel now about drawing with your opposite hand? Learning to draw with your opposite hand is possible and could be fun, but that should not mean that you have to give up drawing with your dominant hand. The goal should be for you to be ambidextrous, not just to draw with your left hand.

If your teacher focused only on your drawing with the opposite hand, she might have low expectations for your ability. However, recognizing that you already draw with one hand and you are now learning to draw with the other puts things in a different perspective. By changing what she focuses on, the teacher can raise her expectations for you and help you be proud of learning to draw with both hands.

You are more than an "LHL" and probably would not appreciate that label. In fact, you would learn to draw better with your left hand if your teacher gave you opportunities to draw with your right hand and praised you for almost being ambidextrous.

Likewise, learning English can be fun, but our goal should be for students to be bi- or multilingual, not only to learn English. Calling students "ELLs" is analogous to calling you an "LHL." The term "ELL" is an example of deficit thinking; it focuses on what students cannot do well—they are not yet good at speaking English. In contrast, the term "emergent bilinguals" is asset thinking or an asset-based term; it recognizes students for their strengths—they already speak one language, and now they are learning another. Let's focus on our students' strengths.

Thus, we will use the term "EBs" instead of "ELLs" for the remainder of the book. Hopefully you too will use this term with your students. As you make an effort to switch from the term "ELLs" to "EBs," it can remind you to also apply the strategies you learn in this book.

## Background on EBs

Even though there are more and more EBs in our classrooms, most of us do not feel prepared to teach them (Lucas, 2011). Following is a discussion on the background of EBs. Before reading this section there are two important points to consider that will be relevant throughout this book.

First, not all EBs are the same—what you read here may or may not be relevant to the EBs in your room. Instead of making assumptions about EBs, it is imperative that you get to know your students. Second, regardless of your students' backgrounds, they can successfully engage in math. The reason for having the discussion that follows is for us to examine our students' strengths and their challenges to determine how we can support them to be successful in math.

Providing students access to the content and developing language is discussed in more detail in chapters 2 and 3. However, there are additional challenges that some EBs experience. There is more to teaching EBs than merely teaching them English and expecting them to improve in all subjects. Not only do EBs have the challenge of learning content in another language but many are also exposed to disadvantages that are not related to language.

About two-thirds of EBs are from low-income families, and this compounds the challenge of learning in another language (Krashen and Brown, 2005). EBs from high social economic status (SES) tend to perform better on tests because they are more likely to have developed academic language in their first language, making it easier for them to learn academic English (Krashen and Brown, 2005). Additionally, parents of EBs from high SES tend to help their students more with homework and have more books in their homes and schools (Feitelson and Goldstein, 1986; Krashen and Brown, 2005).

Unfortunately the schooling that some EBs are receiving is inferior to non-EBs. EBs are more likely to be taught by teachers who have less experience in the classroom and less likely to be taught a rigorous curriculum (Gándara et al., 2003). Furthermore, EBs tend to have fewer resources in schools, even compared to non-EBs from similar SES backgrounds (Gándara et al., 2003).

Of course not all EBs are in poverty, but it is an additional challenge that many EBs face. Paul Gorski (2018), professor at George Mason University, offers teachers strategies to reduce this opportunity gap, but he argues that if we attempt to treat all students the same, the gap will remain. We have to be more equitable with students in poverty. Gorski points out that if a girl is blind, she usually does not have the same access as other students to learning in our schools, so teachers would make accommodations for her. It would not be equitable to treat this girl the same as everyone else.

Gorski (2018) maintains that students in poverty also do not have proper accommodations in our schools and that teachers need to be aware of such inequities and advocate for these students. Like EBs, students of color are disproportionately in poverty (Milner, 2015). Milner says that poverty does not define students but can shape their experiences. The same can be said for EBs. If EBs are in poverty, they may have fewer opportunities, and we need to advocate for them and make the necessary accommodations to reduce the opportunity gaps.

## Background on EBs Learning Math

There is a belief that math is a universal subject and therefore EBs should be able to succeed in this subject without accommodations. Statistics show otherwise. Only 6 percent of EBs in eighth grade are proficient in math, and in 2014 only 63 percent of EBs graduated from high school compared to 82 percent of non-EBs (EDFacts, 2015). Furthermore, not as many EBs are going to college as non-EBs.

Math is a gatekeeper subject. In other words, it separates those who will be successful in school from those who will not. With the increasing importance of education in our society, failing math has dire effects on the future of EBs.

Furthermore, math is changing—there is more language involved (Silver, Saunders, and Zarate, 2008). There is more emphasis on reading math problems and justifying answers. EBs are not doing as well in reading in English, and this influences their achievement in mathematics (August and Shanahan, 2006).

It is not only that EBs are learning math in a second language but also that they are taught math differently from other students, using outdated approaches that lead to lower achievement (Verdugo and Flores, 2007). Decades of research in the field of mathematics education have found that all students should engage in making sense of problems related to their personal lives and persevere to solve them (National Council of Teachers of Mathematics, 2014). We need to learn how to relate mathematics to EBs' personal lives so they can persevere to solve problems (chapter 4).

Despite the challenges mentioned here, we will learn how to engage EBs in math by providing them access to the content and celebrating their differences. As mentioned earlier, we should have the mindset that each student is capable of learning math (Boaler, 2015). For example, instead of focusing on the fact that our students do not speak English well, we can focus on their language expertise for knowing at least one language and learning another. If we learn how to meet the needs of EBs, they can be successful.

## Background on Spanish-Speaking EBs

About 75 percent of the EBs in the United States speak Spanish, and around 70 percent of those are Mexican. Sadly, the climate toward Spanish speakers can be unwelcoming, and this has a strong influence on our students' academic achievement (Valdés and Castellón, 2011). If our students are ignored or not valued, they will not do well in school. If our students are teased and bullied, they will not do well in school. We must advocate for EBs by fighting against the injustices that occur in our schools and society not only because our students will do better academically but also because it is the right thing to do.

Children of parents who do not have permanent status in the United States face additional challenges. Imagine how difficult it is to concentrate on math if you do not know with certainty that your loved ones will be home when you return. Undocumented parents might also be afraid to attend school functions. We need to reassure parents that schools are safe and that we are trustworthy and want the best for their children.

Most of the Spanish-speaking EBs in our schools are born in the United States, but some who have recently arrived have experienced severe hardships, such as walking miles to cross the border or having their homes devastated by hurricanes. While we have to be careful with stereotypes, we also have to be empathetic and ready to assist any students (EBs and non-EBs) who may be experiencing trauma.

We must figure out how to meet the needs of each of our students and know that they can excel. We must focus on the strengths of our students rather than their deficits. Many newcomers have developed resiliency (a highly valued trait) and can excel if we have high expectations for them.

## About This Book

Chapter 1, "Positive Math Mindset," discusses the importance of engaging students' mindsets. Students who have positive math mindsets 1) are passionate about math, 2) believe they can do math if they work hard enough, 3) and are willing to take risks to solve math problems. All students benefit from having positive math mindsets, but this is imperative for Spanish-speaking EBs because instead of learning math in Spanish, they have to learn it in English. The book outlines several strategies to help accomplish this: be culturally relevant, praise the students' efforts, make mathematics fun, and boost relationships.

Chapter 2, "Providing Access," explains how teachers can provide EBs better access to content by choosing tasks with various entry points and using language that is within their zone of proximal development. Techniques such as using graphic organizers, translations, and manipulatives enable Spanish-speaking EBs to solve math problems and have better access to class discussions. Because EBs are more likely to have learned to solve math using algorithms different from ours, being flexible about their choice of algorithm is another way to allow them access to content.

Paradoxically, not only should we provide access to each and every student to solve content but we must also develop their language so they can solve problems in the future. Chapter 3, "Developing Language," emphasizes that teachers need to teach language in math class because today there is more emphasis on students explaining how they solved their answers. By creating a class in which students have ample opportunities to speak in both Spanish and English, we can foster students to develop their language.

Chapter 4, "Productive Struggle," explores the importance of having high expectations for EBs. Students learn mathematics with deeper meaning when they engage in productive struggle—grappling to make sense of problems within their zone of proximal development (Hiebert and Grouws, 2007). Regardless of English proficiency, teachers can still engage EBs in productive struggle by asking more questions and allowing them to discover concepts for themselves rather than telling the answers.

Chapter 5, "Assessment," offers teachers suggestions for giving valid and reliable tests by considering EBs' culture and language. When EBs are given math tests that are grammatically easier to understand, their scores improve (Abedi and Lord, 2001). Fair assessments should be measuring EBs' ability in mathematics, not English proficiency. Equitable strategies for Spanish-speaking EBs are suggested from each of the four chapters: "Positive Math Mindset," "Providing Access," "Developing Language," and "Productive Struggle."

Chapter 6, "Putting It All Together," examines a class of Spanish-speaking EBs who focus on developing positive mindsets, providing access to the content, developing language, and engaging in productive struggle.

The appendices offer additional resources that incorporate the strategies discussed throughout the book. You can refer to the appendices for examples of word problems for Spanish-speaking EBs under the following categories: Positive Math Mindset (Appendix A), Providing Access (Appendix B), Developing Language (Appendix C), Productive Struggle (Appendix D), Assessment (Appendix E), and Putting It All Together (Appendix F). There are also checklists (Appendix G) that you can use to review your understanding of the strategies discussed in the book.

In summary, we need to believe with conviction that each and every student is capable of making sense of problems and solving them. This book is written to help you engage Spanish-speaking EBs. Tweak and adapt the strategies that work best. You will find that many of these strategies will be effective for non-EBs as well. The book offers suggestions on how to engage

Spanish-speaking EBs by developing their positive math mindsets, providing them access to math, developing their language, and engaging them in rigorous, productive math tasks.

Suerte! (Good luck!)

# CHAPTER ONE

~

# Positive Math Mindset

For the upcoming school year, I am looking forward to "spotlighting" a student's culture on a monthly basis. I am hoping to invite a "spokesperson" to come in and introduce us to and educate us on traditions, literature, and customs pertaining to that culture.

My hope is that by creating authentic relationships with my students and their families, I can model that our differences are as normal as our similarities. It is my wish that through these efforts, my students from ALL walks of life feel affirmed and validated in the skin [they're] born in, the traditions they celebrate, the customs they follow, and beliefs that lead their lives.

—Tracie, a tutor for kindergarteners and
first graders, from Spring, Texas

## What Is a Positive Math Mindset?

Too many people believe they aren't good at math and weren't born with a math gene (Boaler, 2015). Research is revealing that such attitudes are ill founded. Evidence indicates that all students can do math—believing in one's capabilities is more important than inherent abilities (Boaler, 2015; Dweck, 2007; Kilpatrick, Swafford, and Findell, 2001).

Students with "positive mindsets in math" understand they can do math not because of their inherited talents but by working hard. These students are more willing to persevere and enjoy challenging tasks. Those with "negative math mindsets" tend to give up more easily and are not as willing to take risks. For the purpose of this book, students who have positive math mindsets 1) are passionate about math, 2) believe they can do math if they work hard enough, 3) and are willing to take risks to solve math problems.

Not only do too many students feel that they are not good at math, there is also a prevalent belief among teachers that some students are not as competent as others. Boaler (2015) reports on a math teacher who believes it is his job to separate the students who are good in math from the ones who are not. He is proud of the way that he "weeds out" the ones who aren't meant to be there. Furthermore, some teachers believe that although we have to be more inclusive and engage all students, certain groups of students—including EBs—are not as capable as others.

All students can develop positive math mindsets. This chapter discusses how to teach Spanish-speaking EBs to do so. Most of the elementary preservice teachers instructed by the author have had negative experiences with math; thus they start an education course with negative math mindsets. The author attempts to change their mindsets by making the math relevant to their lives, offering them specific praise, making math fun, and boosting relationships. When preservice teachers and teachers have positive math mindsets themselves, it is easier for them to develop EBs' mindsets.

As part of the math methods course, preservice teachers go to a local school where they tutor EBs in math. The body language of one student from Mexico revealed that he had not yet acquired a positive math mindset. The college student who worked with him had had negative math experiences herself, but she had made efforts to change. When she asked the boy if he liked math, he shook his head. Before the boy could learn content, the college student would have to develop his math mindset.

The preservice teacher didn't speak Spanish, but she took an interest in the boy's culture and asked him how to say certain words in Spanish. She got to know the boy well and tied the math concepts into his personal life and culture. For each of the six sessions, by praising his effort she attempted to convince him that he was capable of doing the math. At first the boy was afraid to try, but with the college student's patience and caring attitude, the boy opened up. When he made a mistake, she smiled and asked him what he had learned from the mistake. In a few weeks, the boy was enjoying the math activities.

The following semester, a new set of college students worked with the same EBs. The new preservice teachers did not know the students, but the boy, who only four months earlier had had a negative mindset with math, had clearly changed. He smiled, and when asked if he liked math, he said,

"Yes!" He had become more attentive and was willing to take risks. The boy was developing a positive math mindset. Now he enjoys math and knows that if he works hard enough, he is capable of being successful in math.

By developing her own math mindset, even a preservice teacher who had previously had a negative math mindset was able to help this student develop his math mindset.

Because of their situation, many EBs will have to work even harder than non-EBs—not because they are not capable but because they have to learn math in a language that is not native to them while at the same time learning English. All students benefit from having positive math mindsets, but it is imperative for EBs.

No single strategy is likely to be effective for all Spanish-speaking EBs. Just as non-EBs are a diverse population, so are EBs. Spanish-speaking students can be from any race or social class. Most EBs today are born in the United States. Ideally, teachers will develop EBs' positive math mindsets by getting to know each student individually and focusing on each student's strengths. Nevertheless, there are four tools that are found to be generally helpful for teachers. They are to be culturally responsive, to praise effort, to make math fun, and to boost relationships.

## Developing Spanish-Speaking EBs' Positive Math Mindsets

### Culturally Responsive

In the vignette at the beginning of this chapter, Tracie is planning how she will be culturally responsive to meet the needs of her EBs. She wants to celebrate her students' cultures. She argues that being aware of students' differences is not enough—we need to celebrate these differences. Another teacher, Veronica from Corsicana, Texas, connects the math to her students by playing the guitar and singing songs in Spanish. After singing the songs, Veronica asks her students math questions related to the songs.

Nieto (2003) asserts that although education should be based on the premise that all students can learn and deserve the opportunity to do so, not all teachers are relating to their diverse students. When teachers are culturally responsive, EBs' learning improves. Nieto argues that too often teachers engage in the practice of "ethnic tidbits" (p. 8), but teachers need to value students' backgrounds and culture on a daily basis.

Is it unfair to give Spanish-speaking EBs special treatment? On the contrary. Ladson-Billings (2009) argues that it is unfair to attempt to teach everyone the same way. We need to treat each student differently in order to be fair. Thus, applying Ladson-Billings's theory, instead of treating EBs in the same manner as non-EBs, it is both necessary and appropriate to consider each EB student's culture when instructing.

Students are more likely to make sense of problems and persevere to solve them when math is related to their personal lives (Koestler et al., 2013; Clarke et al., 2014). This is often a challenging task for those of us who have backgrounds different from EBs (Howard, 2006; Nieto, 2003), but Kersaint, Thompson, and Petkova (2009) contend that we need to do more than simply replace names used in textbook word problems—they encourage us to connect with EBs by being culturally responsive.

Part of being culturally responsive is to realize how different our students' experiences may have been from our own. Most teachers are white and middle class and are not sure how to meet the needs of EBs. Turner et al. (2012) posit that we need to become familiar with EBs' communities so we can inject what we learn into our math lessons. Valuing multiple strategies in class can aid EBs to engage in math. For example, teachers should be aware that EBs might have learned to solve algorithms differently than have other students (Kersaint, Thompson, and Petkova, 2009).

By creating an inclusive classroom, EBs will feel a sense of belonging in math class and will learn math more deeply while taking chances. Therefore we must create an environment that is culturally responsive in which EBs are open to taking a risk to solve problems. A bonus is that when we are culturally responsive and make an effort to learn how Spanish-speaking EBs solve problems, it can be an enriching experience for the other class members.

*Lesson plans.* We often design lesson plans for non-EBs and then attempt to adapt or "retrofit" these plans for EBs (Ewing, 2018). This practice can be like fitting a square peg into a round hole. Instead we need to accommodate EBs' needs at the planning stage rather than trying to add on to or "retrofit" lessons that have already been designed (Meyer, Rose, and Gordon, 2014). For example, if we take a lesson with a word problem about John buying golf balls at the mall, merely changing the name to Juan may not engage the Spanish-speaking EBs.

At the beginning stages of planning our lessons, we need to consider our EBs' cultures rather than trying to adapt already made lessons to meet their needs. By selecting word problems that reflect EBs' lives and cultures, they will be more likely to take the risk of solving the problems in English. Refer to activity F.2 in appendix F for guidance on how to write lesson plans for Spanish-speaking EBs.

*Culturally responsive books.* One way to facilitate passion and thus improve EBs' math mindsets is by reading culturally responsive books at the beginning of math lessons (Ewing, 2018). Reading children's books at the beginning of

## Textbox 1.1: Summary of Books with Latinx Main Characters

### Round Is a Tortilla by Roseanne Thong

The book hooks all students, including Hispanics, with colorful pictures of children participating in activities. There is a mix of Spanish and English words in this book written for four- to seven-year-olds. This is an excellent way to introduce students to shapes (Ewing, 2018)—students are taught that "abuela's" (grandmother's) pot of stew is round and the "ventanas" (windows) are in the shape of squares.

### ¡Hola! Jalapeño by Amy Wilson Sanger

Although designed for preschoolers, ¡Hola! Jalapeño will engage anyone who likes Mexican food. You can strengthen students' number sense by asking how many olives it would take to make four tostadas and how to make one-third of the guacamole recipe.

### The Night of Las Posadas by Tomie DePaola

Many EBs are born in the United States, and this story for ages four to eight takes place in New Mexico. It could be read during Christmastime and is an example of how many Hispanics still celebrate their holidays and traditions in the United States (Ewing, 2018). As this book is longer, you might want to read part of the book before a measurement lesson and ask the students questions such as the length of Joseph's staff or how long it took to walk the procession (Ewing, 2018).

### Look What Came from Mexico by Miles Harvey

Some students will like this nonfiction book, and it can be a way to introduce a lesson on financial literacy. It is written for seven- to ten-year-olds. Students can calculate the profit they make from selling yucca baskets (Ewing, 2018).

### Sopa de Frijoles/Bean Soup by Jorge Argueta and Rafael Yockteng

Argueta is from El Salvador and writes about Hispanics living in the United States. You have a variety of books by Argueta to choose from about Hispanic food. They are written for elementary students but appeal to all students. His books are written in poetry form in both Spanish and English. Reading the book before a math lesson will engage Hispanics to participate, as they can relate to the Spanish words and food. You may want to tie Argueta's books into topics such as fractions, measurement, and graphs.

math lessons is becoming a popular practice, but we need to choose books that Latinx will relate to. Although we should avoid stereotypes that might offend our EBs, reading a book that they relate to may motivate EBs to engage in the math problems that follow.

Ebe (2010) recommends selecting books that tell about individual characters rather than selecting books that make far-reaching claims about a whole country's culture. Reading culturally responsive books can also help EBs to develop their English proficiency (refer to chapter 3 for more strategies to engage EBs in class discussions). We can ask Latinx in our class whether the experiences of the characters in the books are similar to their experiences.

Textbox 1.1 contains a list of children's books to use at the beginning of a math lesson to engage EBs. The first four are geared toward Mexican Americans and the last one is written by an author from El Salvador. The text that follows each is taken from the article titled "Considering EBs When Planning Lessons."

*Storytelling.* Similar to reading a book at the beginning of math lessons, storytelling can also capture EBs' attention. A kindergarten teacher successfully motivated her students by starting the math class by telling stories about the students' community (Turner et al., 2009). For example, she would tell her students that she bought oranges at a local market where many of her students went shopping.

Turner et al. (2009) found that the students were able to solve more complex mathematic problems when the teacher framed the math concepts around their cultural experiences. In fact, the students were so excited about hearing the teacher tell stories that related to their lives that the Spanish-speaking kindergarten EBs came up with short stories themselves. These stories were converted into word problems involving addition and subtraction.

This same idea can be applied to all grades. Middle school math teachers can tell short stories that EBs can relate to and then tie that story into math. These stories can motivate EBs to solve challenging math problems and help them believe that they can solve word problems if they work hard. There are story starters in textbox 1.2 to which Spanish speakers may relate and that you can adapt to meet the needs of your students. You can tell the stories and add multiple math questions. The stories are left general so they can be used for many grades and math topics.

*Culturally responsive classrooms.* If we are not Latinx, we need to ask ourselves how a Latinx student might feel in our classroom. What is on the walls and bulletin boards? Do we have Spanish words and pictures of Latinx in the classroom? Do the books in the classroom have pictures of Latinx? Please

## Textbox 1.2: Story Starters Appropriate for K–8

1. It is Christmastime and Veronica is excited. Now that she lives in the United States she celebrates Christmas and Santa Claus, but her favorite part of the holiday is still on January 6 (El Dia de los Reyes). She loves eating Rosca de Reyes. The cake is delicious, but the best part is guessing who will get the hidden baby in their slice.

Last year her uncle got the plastic baby in his cake. Everyone says that whoever gets the baby has to host a party on February 2, Dia de la Candelaria—Veronica doesn't think they will make her host a party, but will her slice of cake have the baby? Should she cut a big slice because she likes the Rosca or a small slice so she doesn't get the baby?

2. Manuel loves soccer. His favorite player is Leonardo Messi from Argentina, who plays for the Spanish club team Barcelona. Manuel's friend says that Cristiano Ronaldo is better than Messi. Ronaldo plays for Portugal and used to be on Real Madrid, but now he is on the team Juventus in Italy. Which player is better? How can Manuel decide if Messi is better than Ronaldo?

3. Mariana had so much fun at her sister's *quinceañera* celebration this weekend. The mass was exciting, but Mariana especially liked the waltz afterward. She danced for hours. When she finally stopped dancing, she looked around and counted 275 people at the celebration. How much was it going to cost to feed all of those people? She also wondered how many presents her sister had gotten.

4. Juan wants to help his father cook for his sister's birthday party. Her favorite dessert is arroz con leche. Juan and his father went to the store to buy ingredients. They bought rice, milk, cinnamon, and raisins. But how much of each ingredient should they buy?

5. It was my brother's birthday last week. There were so many relatives at our house because he turned eighteen. I love piñatas, but maybe he is too old and didn't get one. We had a big cake for everyone, and his friends tried to put his head in the cake when he blew out the candles, but he was expecting it so he ran away. Would there be enough cake for everyone at the party?

refer to activity A.1 in appendix A for math activities that tie into Spanish-speaking EBs' foods.

Whenever we pass out manipulatives it is wise to let the students play with them for a minute before using them for the math lesson to "get it out of their system." If they have a minute to play with the manipulatives, they will be less likely to play with them in the middle of the math lesson. Along these lines, before the lesson starts, teachers can have students make the flags of Spanish-speaking EBs with color cubes and then use these colors in the math lesson. For example, Mexican EBs might feel proud using cubes with the colors green, white, and red during a math activity.

*Music.* Research suggests that playing music can boost students' mood and motivate them to be more passionate about learning (Jensen, 2013). We should be purposeful with the music we choose for our students, using energizing music to get the students motivated at the beginning of a lesson and more relaxing music without lyrics when the students are working at their seats. We need to consider students' cultures and play music that our students listen to at home.

We can also develop math problems related to the music by asking questions about the beat, length of the song, or even money made by the Latinx' favorite singers.

*Celebrate successful EBs.* In order for Spanish-speaking EBs to believe that they belong in the world of mathematics, it is crucial that they have role models of successful mathematicians. We can discuss successful mathematicians from the Latinx students' native country and/or culture. After EBs hear about successful mathematicians similar to them, they will believe that they too can be successful. There are videos for children that discuss growth mindsets verses fixed mindsets. We can show those videos about developing positive math mindsets in Spanish.

Learning about neuroscience and neuroplasticity can also help EBs be positive about math—even if they previously thought they were not good at math, this can change. If they watch videos about how people who are like them change their math mindsets, then EBs are encouraged to change their mindsets too.

*Offer opportunities to speak Spanish.* If you don't speak Spanish well and were to move to a Spanish-speaking country, you would find it exhausting to hear Spanish all the time—it would be a relief to occasionally speak in English. Likewise, our Spanish-speaking EBs will enjoy math if we occasionally allow them opportunities to speak and solve problems in their own language.

**Table 1.1.   English/Spanish Math Vocabulary Words**

| English | Spanish |
| --- | --- |
| Add | Sumar |
| Subtract | Restar |
| Multiply | Múltiplicar |
| Divide | Dividir |
| Equals | Igual |
| More | Mas |
| Less | Menos |
| Bigger | Mas grande |
| Smaller | Mas pequeño |
| Number | Número |
| Hundred | Cien |
| Thousand | Mil |
| Line | Línea |
| Square | Cuadrado |
| Triangle | Triángulo |
| Circle | Círculo |
| Perimeter | Perímetro |
| Area | Area |
| Volume | Volumen |
| Graph | Gráfico |
| Fraction | Fracción |
| Decimal | Decimal |
| Why? | Por qué? |
| Speak | Habla |
| Even or odd? | Par o impar? |
| True | Verdad |
| Slope | Pendiente |
| The mean | La media |
| Constant | Constante |
| Integer | Número entero |

We can accept code switching (mixing two languages). While our goal is for EBs to be proficient in English, at times we need to focus more on EBs' math proficiency.

Chapter 3 will discuss developing EBs' English proficiency, but if there is too much emphasis on this, EBs may feel they are not good at math because the teacher is always correcting them. In table 1.1 there is a list of math words in English and a corresponding list in Spanish. Even if you have limited Spanish proficiency, you can use the vocabulary words to initiate a conversation with Spanish-speaking students. Please note that to make this simpler, the articles are not included in the table.

**Praise Efforts**

We should never tell students they are smart or good at math—that only pro-motes the belief that some have the "math gene" and others do not (Boaler, 2015). It is rare to hear someone say that they don't read, and yet we seem to think it is acceptable for people to say that they don't do math or aren't good at math. We want to get away from that idea. All students can do math. We want our students to take risks in math and believe that they can do math by working hard. If there is too much focus on getting the right answer, some students may give up. By focusing on students' efforts, all students, including EBs, can succeed in math.

*Appreciate EBs' efforts for learning math in a second language.* EBs have the challenging task of learning math and English at the same time. This deserves recognition from the teacher and the other students. It is especially intimidating for EBs who are not proficient in English to express their math-ematical ideas with peers who are native speakers. Imagine how you would feel if you had to explain a math concept in another language. By being empathetic, we can boost EBs' confidence in their ability to do math.

Thus, we can be patient with EBs for making mistakes and focus more on their math ideas than on their incorrect English grammar. Sometimes we spend so much time correcting EBs' grammar that the students shut down or are embarrassed. Moschkovich (2007) cites how one student mispronounced the word "rectangle" but still developed a mathematical argument by using gestures.

Moschkovich (2007) reasons that by praising the student for her math skills, the student is more likely to continue to take chances. This author believes if mathematics is limited to defining terms, EBs will always be at a disadvantage. She points out that EBs are more likely to take risks if they are allowed to use gestures, occasionally speak in their own language, and use manipulatives or objects while they are expressing their ideas. It is beneficial to encourage students to take risks; countries that perform the best on inter-national math tests take more risks (Boaler, 2015; Dweck, 2007).

*Avoid saying "good job" and "good effort."* Merely saying "good job" is not effective for any student. After receiving this compliment, EBs will not know why we are praising them. It is much better to be specific and tell EBs exactly what we like about their mathematical practices—that way they understand our expectations. Many teachers constantly say "good job" and waste the opportunity to offer specific feedback. At first we may find it difficult to break the habit, so when we catch ourselves saying "good job," we can add what specifically was good about the student's performance.

Dweck (2015), the researcher who first developed the growth mindset concept, cautions that some teachers have not fully understood her idea of praising effort. Having a growth or math mindset is more than blindly telling students they can do it. She found teachers who would observe students solving problems ineffectively but who nevertheless praised them for their effort.

Dweck (2015) claims some teachers are saying "good effort" with the hope that students will develop that mindset, but these empty praises were not helpful—students could detect the lack of sincerity. The researcher argues for teachers to limit praising students' efforts to when they are using effective strategies that promote conceptual development. Thus, we should send the message that it is okay to make mistakes, but if EBs are working on ineffective math strategies, we should eventually redirect them. It is effective to praise EBs with specific feedback when they truly work hard and develop effective strategies.

While we should praise EBs' efforts when they are on the right track, they will be even more motivated if we offer specific feedback and add to our praise our students' goals (Frey, Hattie, and Fisher, 2018). If we get to know our EBs, we can tell them that if they continue to work hard, they can achieve their goals. Textbox 1.3 offers two specific praises that you might give to your Spanish-speaking EBs.

### Textbox 1.3: Specific Praise

"Isabela, I like the way you persevered to solve the second math problem. If you continue like this, it will help you with your goal of being an engineer." "Jose Luis, I am in awe of how you keep trying to sound out all of those word problems. I can't imagine myself solving word problems in Spanish!" (Refer to chapter 3 for adapting teacher talk according to EBs' proficiency level.)

### Make Math Fun

Students tend to love math in kindergarten and learn to hate it as they get older. In the younger grades math tends to be more engaging, relevant, and more of a game. If we want our EBs to be passionate about math, we need to make it fun.

*Be passionate about math ourselves.* If we want our students to be passionate about math, we too should be passionate. Because they don't have English proficiency, EBs focus on nonverbal communication and will be especially aware of the degree to which teachers enjoy math.

Kilpatrick, Swafford, and Findell (2001) maintain that if teachers themselves are more excited about math, then their students will be too. Furthermore, if students have positive math mindsets, this disposition can carry on into their adult lives (National Council of Teachers of Mathematics, 2014). Thus, we need to be excited about math and encourage EBs to view themselves as capable mathematicians.

*Avoid "traditional math."* Many students are drilled in mathematics, but this is especially the case for EBs. Perhaps because teachers feel they cannot communicate with them, math for EBs is often limited to worksheets and drills. Drilling students can be negative and, although it is intended to improve speed, drilling does not promote students' love of math. We want to de-emphasize the belief that good mathematicians are fast. Instead of going fast, it is better to encourage students to persevere at solving problems.

Mathematics needs to have a purpose and context. At the NCTM conference in 2019, the keynote speaker, Dr. Ladson-Billings, argued that mathematics needs context. She said that three plus four does not always equal seven—it could equal three. If there were three snakes and four mice, there would be a total of three animals if they were in the same vicinity—not seven (the snakes would eat the mice). Her point was that if we drill our students in arithmetic without a context, mathematics does not always make sense to our students.

In order to empathize with EBs who are given what for them is senseless arithmetic without context, refer to figure 2.1 in chapter 2. There is a worksheet that asks you to solve math the way it is done in most Latin countries. However, there is no context—it is pure arithmetic. Imagine what it would be like to solve problems like those in the worksheet in figure 2.1 (Ewing, 2017).

_Play math games._ Math games can boost EBs' enjoyment of the subject and typically do not require much teacher preparation time or money (Ferlazzo and Sypnieski, 2018). Furthermore, games can motivate EBs to develop their English proficiency because there is typically a focus on student-student discourse as opposed to teachers lecturing about content (chapter 3). Refer to activity C.2 in appendix C for games to play with Spanish-speaking EBs.

*Math and movement.* EBs tend to like kinesthetic approaches to learning. Instead of sitting at our desks, we can learn math through movement. For example, instead of attempting to solve a number line on a worksheet, math can come alive when we make a number line out of the students in the class.

Another example would be to make a "living graph" of students—students could simulate a bar graph by getting in rows.

*Brain breaks.* It is tiring to learn math and English at the same time. Even a minute break for students to move around can provide access. After taking a break, EBs (and non-EBs) will be more likely to continue working on math. Of course, whenever possible, we can play music that our EBs can relate to. Please refer to activity A.2 in appendix A for culturally responsive brain breaks for Spanish-speaking EBs.

Playing with balloons serves as a short break and develops class community. Students can be put in groups of four to six and each group blows up a balloon. The rules are for each group to hold hands and keep the balloon up in the air. When students get good at this activity, more balloons can be added. This activity may sound easy, but the challenge is that students have to work together as they hold hands. After doing this activity, the teacher can ask math questions related to balloons.

*Include math projects.* Instead of the popular science fairs, you can put on a "geometry fair." All students, including the EBs, enjoy this activity, and it promotes students' love of math. Not only are geometry fairs hands-on, but learning geometry for students seems different from "regular math." Begin by having students draw colorful two-dimensional shapes and classify them. Then do the same with three-dimensional figures.

After a week of experimenting with shapes, the students are assigned a project involving geometry. Instead of making the projects at home, students should design their projects in class. Planning a project with a partner or a small group is especially valuable for the EBs because they have opportunities to develop their English proficiency. There are a variety of projects that students can teach.

When students obtain expertise in geometry, they share their projects with other classes in the cafeteria or wherever there is space in your school. One group can make colorful circle patterns with a compass and ask the visiting students questions about chords, diameters, and the area of circles. Then the students can teach the other students how to make the circular patterns.

A second group can learn about quadrilaterals and teach "Quadrilateral Concentration." After learning about quadrilaterals, the visiting students are asked to turn over cards and match the shape with the correct definitions. A third group makes board games and asks the other students questions about geometry. The geometry fair is engaging for EBs. There are lots of visuals and they have many opportunities to develop their English by explaining concepts to other students.

Another option is to put on a "measurement fair." Similar to a geometry fair, this fair is fun for students. One group of students makes a paper airplane and asks the visiting students to predict how far an airplane will fly. Then the students measure the distance with rulers. Another group has scales and asks students to predict the mass of various toys. We can boost EBs' confidence by making them the experts in the measurement fair. These projects can be adapted for any grade level and are engaging for all students, including EBs.

Instead of sitting at their desks filling out worksheets in silence, these activities develop EBs' positive math mindsets. Furthermore, these activities push students to develop their English proficiency while simultaneously developing math concepts. Asking questions is a difficult task for EBs, so typically teachers ask the questions and students answer. However, activities that involve students asking other students questions can be especially beneficial for EBs who need this practice.

**Boost Relationships**
The fourth strategy for developing EBs' math mindsets is boosting relationships. John Hattie (2009) has researched the most effective practices for teachers and boosting relationships with students is high on the list. When we boost relationships with EBs, they will be more likely to enjoy math. Students work harder for teachers that they like, and when teachers get to know their students well, they can ask them problems that capitalize on their strengths. We should boost relationships with our students, class, and parents.

*Focus on EBs' assets, not deficits.* We can develop positive math mindsets by focusing on what students have to offer instead of what they are lacking. Instead of focusing on EBs' lack of English proficiency, we can focus on their mathematical assets. EBs will develop the belief that they are capable in math if you use them as a resource.

We can look for EBs' assets in areas such as the metric system. The majority of EBs have grown up in the United States and will not necessarily have a stronger grasp of the metric system than their peers, but others have learned about the metric system from their families or home country. We can enhance students' math mindsets by making them the experts and teaching other students about the metric system (Kersaint, Thompson, and Petkova, 2009).

We can also be flexible and praise EBs for solving problems in a different way from the other students. Peers of EBs may make the false assumption that they are not competent in math when they lack sophisticated mathematical arguments. If this happens, we can revoice EBs' ideas and ask the rest of the class to consider EBs' mathematical arguments. By focusing on their assets, EBs can have a stronger conviction that they are capable mathematicians.

*Pronounce students' names correctly.* Other students will imitate our pronunciation of names. EBs' peers mispronounce names as a result of the teacher's mistake. Names are related to identity and pronouncing them correctly will boost students' passion for learning. Of course, there are exceptions. One teacher pronounced a student's name as "Daniel" in English instead of Spanish. The boy wanted to have that pronunciation to be "American."

Some EBs strive to fit in and be accepted by their classmates and attempt to be "American" by assimilating to their new culture. Obviously, you need to honor the student's preference when you find out what it is. However, if you value multiculturalism, EBs may be prouder of their names and culture.

*Interview students.* Find the time to talk to Spanish-speaking EBs. This will not only be an opportunity to boost their language (chapter 3) but will also be an opportunity to boost your relationship with them. You can ask their favorite hobbies, interests, and goals. Then you can design some of your math problems around their interests. You can also motivate students to persevere with solving the problems if you tie your encouragement into their goals. For example, "Alberto, if you continue working so hard on those problems, it will help you with your goal of being a math teacher."

*Learn about backgrounds.* As mentioned earlier, not all EBs are the same. We need to know, for example, if they were born in the United States or abroad. If we get to know our EBs we can focus on their strengths and include math word problems that engage them. It is imperative to get to know EBs' previous educational experiences. For those students who were born in another country, we can investigate how those countries typically solve math. There are multiple algorithms for division and subtractions, and we should be flexible and allow multiple strategies for solving problems.

*Be especially nice to the newcomers.* It is important to be nice to each student, but we need to pay special attention to newcomers (EBs who have just arrived to our country). We can talk to the class and make sure everyone is kind to the newcomers and assign a student who speaks Spanish to make sure they are having fun in the cafeteria and at recess. With time, the newcomers will adapt to and be part of the class, but at first, we need to build the trust. We can also assign a Spanish speaker to help the newcomers have access to the content (chapter 2).

We may need to explain to the newcomers the class rules. They will need to have the homework policy explained and be taught how to ask to go to the bathroom. This may be irrelevant to teaching math, but it is hard to concentrate on math if you are trying to figure out how to ask to go to the bathroom. If the teacher is nice to the newcomers, then the other students will be too, and they will be more integrated and accepted.

*Avoid grouping by ability.* EBs are typically "held back" in math due to their lack of English proficiency. Unfortunately, if they are put in "lower math groups," EBs stuck in the same track may come to believe they don't have a math gene. If EBs are put in a lower track, they may not like math and thus not develop a positive math mindset. San Francisco no longer tracks their students until tenth-grade algebra, and the students are doing much better—when they are tracked, the students in lower tracks have negative math mindsets.

*Respect the silent period.* When acquiring a second language, it is typical to go through a silent period at the beginning stages. This is a natural process, and we need to respect EBs who choose not to talk. After EBs go through the silent phase, it will be important to develop their math language, but as EBs are adapting to their new environment, they should be allowed to remain silent.

*Build relationships with parents.* Some teachers complain that parents of EBs do not come to parent-teacher conferences, and it is challenging to get to know parents due to language barriers. However, it can be done. If we go through the extra step to write a letter in another language or invite parents to attend morning meetings, their children will be happier and will prosper.

### Textbox 1.4: Simple Phrases for Parent Conferences

1. I am happy/worried about your son's/daughter's progress. (Estoy contenta/o/ preocupada/o con el progreso de su hijo/hija.)

2. Your son/daughter likes math. (A su hijo/hija le gustan las matemáticas.)

3. Can you please make sure that he/she does more math homework? (Por favor, su hijo/hija debe hacer más tareas de las matemáticas.)

4. Your son/daughter participates in class discussions. (Su hijo/hija participa en nuestras conversaciones de matemáticas.)

5. Now we are studying about . . . in math class. (Ahora estamos estudiando . . . en clase de las matematicas.)

When we build relationships with parents, they will be a bigger part of the learning community and can even help their students with math homework. Some schools offer Latin dancing in the evenings to encourage parents to come to school. This is welcoming for parents and offers the opportunity for parents who know how to dance to be the experts and even instruct teachers and other parents.

In textbox 1.4 there are some simple phrases in Spanish that you might want to use during parent-teacher conferences. Even if you are not fluent in Spanish, parents will appreciate the effort you make to speak a few phrases in Spanish. Please note that if you are female, you would say "contenta" and if you are male you would use "contento."

## Key Ideas for Developing Positive Math Mindsets

- All students benefit from having a positive math mindset—a belief that they can do math if they work hard, are passionate about math, and are willing to take risks.
- EBs learn math in another language, so they will have to work even harder; they will especially benefit from having a positive math mindset.
- EBs are more likely to be passionate about math if we relate math to their personal lives and if we are culturally responsive.
- Our appreciation of EBs' efforts to learn both math and English at the same time will make them more willing to keep trying and take risks.
- Too many EBs are drilled in math, and that makes math boring. Alternatively, we can make math fun and encourage EBs to be passionate about math.
- By boosting our relationships with EBs, they will be more likely to take risks in math and enjoy it.
- In the following chapters we will discuss more strategies to help EBs in math, but these strategies will only be effective if our students develop positive math mindsets.
- Please refer to activity G.1 in appendix G for a self-assessment of the key ideas in this chapter.

CHAPTER TWO

# Providing Access

As a new teacher, teaching math to ELLs seemed daunting at first, but it was easier than I expected. Teaching any kind of lesson to an ELL, be it math, reading, writing, or science, is similar to teaching a lesson to a student whose first language is English. The difference is the support systems or manipulatives you have to have available.

Just like many other students in the classroom, my third-grade ELL student used the method that made the most sense to him, partial products. So I made time to pull a small group, my ELL included, to teach a mini-lesson on partial products using base ten-block manipulatives as needed. This student knew his single-digit multiplication but could not grasp double-digit until we sat down in that small group. He learned double-digit multiplication using partial products and base ten blocks in one day. He was even able to teach other students in the class how to use partial products!

—Anna, third-grade student teacher from Crockett, Texas

## What Is Providing Access?

Students cannot solve math problems unless they have access to them. Ladson-Billings (2009), a famous education researcher for social justice, says that we shouldn't treat all students the same. She explains that we would not force students in a wheelchair to do push-ups in PE class just because everyone else is doing them, so why treat everyone the same?

When teaching mathematics, we should meet each student's needs, and this is different from treating all students equally (National Council of Teachers of Mathematics, 2014). The council suggests that we accommodate each student's needs so that all students can be successful in math.

Koestler et al. (2013) propose that we provide access to students by choosing math problems for our students with multiple entry points. Because every student is different, if we select open tasks, more students can solve our problems. For example, we should offer fewer traditional problems that have only one answer and often only a few strategies to solve them.

When tasks are closed, some students will finish early while others will struggle to complete the problems. Alternatively, we can choose open tasks relevant to our students' lives that can be solved in various ways.

## Providing Access for Spanish-Speaking EBs

In the epigraph at the beginning of the chapter, a student teacher, Anna, described her approach for providing access to an EB student. She realized that he was not grasping multiplication of two digits, so she taught a small group the concept. After a short session using manipulatives, the student was able to do the math and even taught his peers.

Often EBs are capable of doing the math we assign them but struggle with the linguistic and cultural barriers. All students, including EBs, need access to engage in math. In order to understand how EBs may feel when solving math problems, imagine the following math problem in textbox 2.1.

What challenges might Spanish-speaking EBs have solving the problem in textbox 2.1? Many. There might be some vocabulary challenges, such as "mall," "pairs," and "show." The word "pair" is a homophone and may be confused with the word "pear." Likewise, the word "show" might trip up some students because they may be used to TV shows. Therefore we have to be careful EBs understand homophones in math problems.

### Textbox 2.1: A Math Problem That Is Not Culturally Responsive

"John went to the mall to buy some clothes. If he bought 3 pairs of pants and each pair cost $32, how much did he have to pay? Please show your work."

### Textbox 2.2: A Math Problem in Spanish

"Marcos compra muchos jugetes para sus nietos El Dia de Reyes. Si su sobrino compra una dozena y el abuelo compra la mitad, cuantos regalos compra Marcos? Como resolviste el problema?"

Apart from vocabulary challenges, this is a problem that may not be culturally responsive to all. Some EBs in our classrooms are not used to going to the mall to shop. For a start, you need a car to get to the mall. Some students would be used to shopping at marketplaces. Ninety-six dollars is also a lot of money for some children, and they might not relate this problem to their personal lives. Last, students may be able to solve the problem in Spanish but not have the English proficiency to explain how they arrived at the solution.

To give you an idea of what many EBs experience when learning both English and math at the same time, please solve the problem in Spanish in textbox 2.2 without looking at the translation, which is in textbox 2.3.

How did you feel if you are not fluent in Spanish and tried to solve the problem? Often teachers attempt to help EBs solve math problems by merely including students' names, but would you have had access to the problem if I had used your name instead of Marcos? Hopefully, after attempting to solve this problem in Spanish, you have more empathy for EBs who solve math problems in English instead of Spanish. Now look at textbox 2.3, which is a translation of the math problem in Spanish.

Similar to EBs, you may have recognized some words but not made meaning of the whole problem. For example, the word "Reyes" might have been confusing to you because it usually means "kings," but in this sentence it means "Wise Men" and is referring to January 6, when Latin countries

### Textbox 2.3: A Translation of the Math Problem from Textbox 2.2

"Marcos buys a lot of toys for his grandchildren for 'Kings' Day.' (This is on January 6 and when many children receive presents in Latin countries.) If his nephew buys a dozen (of toys) and the grandfather bought half as many, how many toys did Marcos buy? Show how you solved the problem."

celebrate Christmas. As mentioned earlier, it can be confusing when words have more than one meaning.

To further empathize how EBs may feel learning math in English, attempt to solve the worksheet (figure 2.1). Imagine you are in a classroom and all of the instructions are in Spanish. The teacher does not use gestures and speaks very fast. You don't understand the instructions and suddenly the teacher plops a sheet on your desk.

You do not know what the questions are asking. You resourcefully take out your phone and proceed to translate the directions, but the teacher signals that phones are not allowed in the class. You politely and timidly explain in English to the teacher that you do not understand what to do. The teacher answers you in Spanish and you are still confused. Then the teacher leaves to answer another student's question and you are on your own to solve the problems. What would you do? How would you feel? With this scenario in mind, attempt to solve the questions in figure 2.1.

How did you feel? Teachers typically report that after solving these problems they felt "frustrated," "stupid," "angry," and "afraid." Figure 2.1 was asking you to divide. This is how division is done in most countries in South America and in Spain. You may have thought before attempting to solve these problems that "math is math." There is no language involved.

| Las Matemáticas | | | Nombre .................... |
|---|---|---|---|
| *1:* | *2:* | *3:* | *4:* |
| 1485 $\mid$ 45 | 5525 $\mid$ 85 | 4592 $\mid$ 56 | 18.936 $\mid$ 24 |
| *5:* | *6:* | *7:* | *8:* |
| 15.375 $\mid$ 125 | 10.870 $\mid$ 110 | 11.700 $\mid$ 180 | 12.615 $\mid$ 87 |

**Figure 2.1. Solving Math in Spanish**
Ewing, J. (2017). Facilitating pre-service teachers to learn the Mathematical Practices and engage English language learners. *The Journal of Multicultural Affairs, 2*(1), 1–5.

However, you probably did not solve the problems, not because you don't know how to divide but because you didn't have access to the problems.

Furthermore, look at problems number 4 to number 8. What is being asked of you? You may think that the problems have decimals in them, but periods in Latin countries are used to separate digits like we use commas. Number 4 is asking you to divide 18,936 by 24, not 18.936 by 24.

Even though you know this is a simulation, how might EBs feel solving math in English in your classroom? Can it be done? Yes, but we must provide our EBs with access to the content. Reflect on how *you* could have had access to solve the problems from figure 2.1.

First of all, consider if you were hooked into solving the problems even if you had understood the directions. The sheet was simply plopped on your desk and there was no hook for you to solve the problems. Did you have a purpose or motivation for solving the problems? Would you be motivated to persevere to solve these problems or would you ask yourself, "If I can do one, what is the point of doing eight tedious problems?" How would you feel if one of your peers finished while you were barely getting started? Did the teacher consider you and your interests when assigning these problems?

Would it have helped if your teacher had met with you individually for a few minutes before the math lesson? Your teacher could have explained that you were going to do division and that the word sounds the same in Spanish (división). Also, if your teacher had spoken slowly and used gestures, you might have had better access to the math.

In the past, in math class students were typically given worksheets and asked to solve problems. However, today there is more emphasis on solving word problems. How can we provide EBs access to our math lessons to limit the frustration that you may have felt when solving the problems in figure 2.1? Following are some strategies for you to use before and during lessons to provide EBs with access to math problems so they can be successful in your class. The strategies are divided into four groups: planning, warm-up, speaking to EBs, and scaffolding tips during the lesson.

**Planning Lessons**

If we are going to successfully meet the needs of our students, we need to plan for them in advance. Typically lessons are planned for non-EBs and there are notes for the teacher in the margin to adapt the lesson for EBs. This does not always work. Instead of trying to adapt already-made lesson plans for EBs, we should think of meeting their cultural and linguistic needs from the beginning. Refer to activity F.2 in appendix F for guidance on writing lesson plans for Spanish-speaking EBs.

*Hook?* How will you motivate your students to access the problems? How can the math problems be introduced in a fun away for the EBs? Are the math problems and lesson culturally responsive for the EBs?

*Write clear content and language goals.* You should know the language and math concept goals for each lesson, and they should be posted. More importantly, EBs should know the goals for the lesson. They need to be clear about the "why" or purpose of each lesson.

*Differentiation.* It is important to plan how to best meet the varying language needs of each Spanish-speaking EB. For example, plan before the lesson what visuals you will use so each student can access the content. Will you bring in real objects, use pictures and videos to help EBs have access to the math, or simply talk? What questions are you planning to ask each EB student to better engage each one throughout the lesson?

*Drills or higher-level thinking?* Do the EBs have access to engage in high-level thinking or are they just being drilled? Too often EBs are drilled more than non-EBs. Remember how you felt being drilled when trying to solve the problems from figure 2.1.

*Enough time?* EBs typically need more time to solve math problems in a second language. How will you plan the lesson to afford EBs ample time?

*Work with the ESL teacher.* Let the ESL teacher know how she might be able to support your students in math. You may consider giving her vocabulary words that she can review with your students. Typically ESL teachers have a strong literacy and ELA background but do not have much training in math. It may be necessary to spend some time with the ESL teacher explaining how you teach math and how she can help each Spanish-speaking EB in math.

## Warming-Up Exercises Before Solving

Instead of waiting for students to fail, it is much better to be proactive and predict how to help EBs have access to the content by doing warm-up exercises before the lesson starts. Here are some strategies.

*Priming.* It is effective to tell EBs what they will be learning the day before or even minutes before the actual lesson. For example, you can tell EBs that the next day they will be learning a lesson about linear equations. An example of priming is preteaching key vocabulary words so EBs are more prepared on the day of the lesson.

*Develop background knowledge.* Before students start solving problems, we should ask questions to get them interested. If EBs are going to solve word problems about a zoo, we need to know which students have experienced going to the zoo. We often take for granted that our students have had such experiences, but if they haven't, they are at a disadvantage solving these

**Textbox 2.4: Sentence Stems for KWL Charts at the Zoo**

I know that _____ are about _____ feet tall.
I want to know how much _____ weigh.
I learned that _____ are taller than _____.

problems. We can give students the context of the problems and explain cultural contexts that may be necessary to solve the problems.

KWL (What a student Knows, Wants to know, and has Learned about a topic) charts are effective because they visually point out what the students know and what they want to learn. The only caveat with KWL charts is at times teachers ask the whole class what they know and a few dominant students fill out the charts for the class. Help EBs by taking the time to find out what they specifically know about the topics. Textbox 2.4 has examples of sentence stems that can support EBs to share what they know, want to know, and have learned.

*Develop vocabulary.* Depending on EBs' English and reading proficiency, it may be effective for teachers to skim the text first with them. Instead of immediately asking which words the EBs do not understand, we can be proactive and ask which words they recognize. Vocabulary should be taught but should not be limited to drilling. We should also have patience with our students and avoid teaching them more than two new words per lesson. We will also need to repeat the new words throughout the lesson.

*Teach cognates.* There are many words that have similar meanings in two languages. We used to think that EBs had to start using English from the beginning, but now we realize the importance of helping EBs make the transfer from one language to another (Cummins, 1981). If EBs are taught that a "triangle" is a cognate with "triangulo," they do not have to learn that new concept if they already know the concept in their own language. Learning cognates will help them make the transfer. In table 2.1 you can refer to a list of math cognates in English and Spanish.

**Teacher Talk to EBs during the Lesson**

Teachers tend to talk too much. We need to have mathematical conversations with students, including EBs, rather than lecturing (Kersaint, Thompson, and Petkova, 2009). In this manner, students will listen closely because they know that they will have opportunities to talk later in the lesson. Following are some guidelines for you to refer to when speaking to EBs so they can understand you and have better access to the content.

**Table 2.1.  Math Cognates in English and Spanish**

| English | Spanish |
|---|---|
| Algebra | Algebra |
| Angle | Angulo |
| Arc | Arco |
| Area | Área |
| Bar graph | Gráfico de barras |
| Base | Base |
| Calculate | Calcular |
| Capacity | Capacidad |
| Circle | Circulo |
| Common factor | Factor común |
| Cone | Cono |
| Cube | Cubo |
| Cylinder | Cilíndro |
| Data | Datos |
| Decimal | Decimal |
| Denominator | Denominador |
| Discount | Discuento |
| Double | Doble |
| Equilateral triangle | Triángulo equilátero |
| Estimation | Estimación (mas o menos) |
| Exponent | Exponente |
| Factor | Factor |
| False | Falso |
| Formula | Formula |
| Fraction | Fracción |
| Function | Función |
| Graph | Grafica |
| Line | Línea |
| Math | Matemáticas |
| Million | Millón |
| Multiple | Múltiple |
| Parallel | Paralelo |
| Perpendicular | Perpendicular |
| Polygon | Polígano |
| Probability | Probabilidad |
| Proportion | Proporción |
| Radius | Radio |
| Rectangle | Rectángulo |
| Scale | Escala |
| Simplify | Simplificar |
| Solution | Solución |
| Statistic | Estadística |
| Triangle | Triangulo |
| Volume | Volumen |

*Gestures.* Point. Yes, point! Not to people, but it is easier for EBs to follow along if we use gestures and point to objects that we are talking about. Using our fingers when we count will help a lot. Have you ever watched Latinx talking on the phone? It is a stereotype, but they often use gestures even on the phone. Using gestures helps communicate ideas with all EBs but might be especially important for Latinx.

*Repetition.* Constant repetition and review will help, especially with oral communication.

*Avoid using idioms, pronouns, and jokes.* Understanding idioms, pronouns, and jokes is challenging for students learning a second language. While laughing can reduce the stress for EBs, if they do not understand what is going on, they can feel left out.

*Slowly.* Have you ever listened to a conversation in another language? It seems like they are speaking so fast! Let's consider this as we are speaking to our students. Depending on their proficiency level, EBs will benefit from extra processing time. At the beginning stages, EBs may be translating the math into Spanish, and this takes time.

*Simple.* Use short and simple sentences and grammar at the beginning stages.

*Expressive.* Because EBs may not understand each word that you say, they will focus on other skills to understand your messages. Be expressive to keep their attention.

*Smile.* Even if EBs do not understand each word we say, we can boost their attention span by smiling.

Textbox 2.5 is an acronym to help remember how to speak to EBs.

## Textbox 2.5: Acronym for Remembering How to Speak to Students

*Remember GRASSES when speaking to EBs:*

Gestures
Repeat
Avoid idioms, puns, and jokes
Speak slowly
Simple sentences
Expressive
Smile

## Scaffolding Tricks for Providing Access

The following tricks may be useful for non-EBs but are imperative for EBs. These strategies are helpful because they have strong visual and language components.

*Visuals.* If you have been to a workshop on how to meet the needs of EBs, there was probably a strong focus on the use of visuals. Yes, use visuals to provide access for EBs. Drawings are visual and should be encouraged when solving math problems. EBs will have more access to solve problems if you draw pictures in your explanations and encourage students to do the same (Hufferd-Ackles, Fuson, and Sherin, 2004).

*Use pictures and photographs.* If we want EBs to use pictures to solve problems, we should model by accompanying our explanations with pictures and photographs too. Furthermore, the pictures we choose should be culturally responsive to hook our EBs. If we can't find pictures related to EBs' culture, at least we can include pictures that are school related—these pictures help level the playing field. Math problems can also be solved in cartoon format—the math can be just as challenging, but EBs will have more access. The saying that a picture is worth a thousand words is accurate—especially for EBs.

*Graphic organizers.* These are visual structures such as charts, graphs, and Venn diagrams. Graphic organizers are easier for students to read than just text. There are a variety of ways these can be used when EBs learn math. You can make graphic organizers at the beginning of a topic to help students see the relationship between words.

The example in table 2.2 can be adapted to any grade and topic. The teacher only has to write in the math terms for the EBs. By looking at the drawing or example, the teacher can instantly decide if the student has grasped the concept. Once the student gets used to completing these sheets, he or she can complete the chart for the words he or she does not understand on his or her own. This graphic organizer will give the students a rich understanding of math terms and they can reference their lists during math class. Please refer to activity B.2 in appendix B for more graphic organizers.

Teachers could make graphic organizers for all of their students. As the teacher is teaching a new unit, she can provide an organizer for her students to help them organize their thoughts. For example, if the class is learning about a topic for a week, the students can be given a graphic organizer like in table 2.2. If students get a chance to write down their ideas at the end of each lesson, their brains will be ready to learn something new the next day. Too often we do not give students opportunities to process information.

There are multiple uses for graphic organizers like the one in table 2.3. Students can fill it out before a lesson so the teacher can learn their

**Table 2.2. A Graphic Organizer**

| Palabra en Español | Word in English | Significado en Español | Meaning in English | Dibujo/ Drawing or Ejemplo/ Example |
|---|---|---|---|---|
| | Proper fraction | | | |
| | Improper fraction | | | |
| | Mixed number | | | |
| | Ratio | | | |
| | Proportion | | | |
| | Decimal | | | |
| | Percent | | | |

background knowledge for each concept, fill it out in pairs at the end of a unit, or use it for review.

As students become skilled at using graphic organizers, it is effective to ask students to make their own. This not only promotes deep mathematical thinking as students look for patterns but can also give teachers feedback on student understanding. A teacher could ask the student to draw quadrilaterals in order (hierarchy). If a student were to draw something like what is shown in figure 2.2, the teacher can determine that the EBs have a grasp of the concept even if they write the terms in Spanish. Using graphic organizers is beneficial for all students but imperative for EBs.

**Table 2.3. Another Graphic Organizer**

Fill in the boxes with pictures, explanations, and/or examples (rellena los espacios).

| Comparing Fractions | Reducing Fractions |
|---|---|
|  |  |
| Adding Fractions | Subtracting Fractions |
|  |  |

*Use manipulatives and realia.* Maldonado et al. (2009) found that using manipulatives allowed EBs to have better access to class discussions. Not only could the EBs better develop math arguments with manipulatives, they also could understand their peers better when they used them. Often teachers allow the use of manipulatives during the discovery part of the lesson but take them away at the end of the lesson because they don't want students to distract others by playing with manipulatives during class discussions.

EBs should have access to manipulatives and realia throughout the lesson so they have more access to mathematical discussions. Math can come alive if we use hula-hoops for circles and Venn diagrams rather than merely drawing circles. Real objects such as food, books, and clothing that relate to EBs' lives can be more motivating for them. For Mexican EBs, using frijoles as counters may stimulate interest.

Ideally we should use objects that relate to EBs' personal lives. Another option to help level the playing field is allowing students to graph objects from the classroom. When teachers have students make and interpret graphs of objects that they are not familiar with, it is boring and harder to understand. All students will benefit from using manipulatives and realia that they can relate to, but this is imperative for EBs.

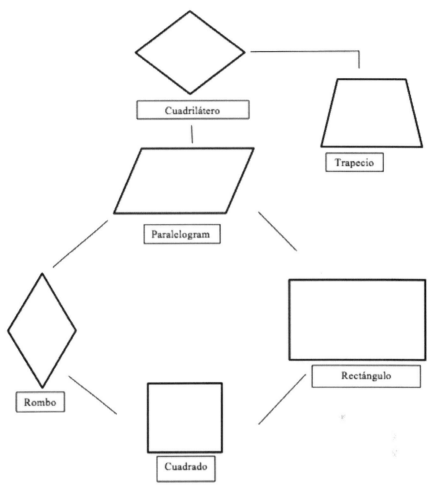

**Figure 2.2.   An Example of a Student's Graphic Organizer**

*Sentence starters/stems.* Sentence starters give EBs opportunities to both better understand their peers and to speak. Coggins (2014) explains that the goal of the class should be to hear all students' arguments. She says that by offering sentence starters, EBs who would ordinarily lack the English proficiency to participate in whole class discussions can be supported to do so.

Sentence starters can also be used in small group discussions to help all students feel that their ideas are valued. Including pictures can be an additional support for Spanish-speaking students who need it. As shown in textbox 2.6, sentence stems should be more open as EBs improve their English

## Textbox 2.6: Math Sentence Stems

*Sentence stems for EBs with limited English proficiency:*
"Miguel had _____ empanadas and he gave _____ to his friends. How many empanadas does Miguel have now?"

*Sentence stems for EBs with advanced English proficiency:*
"Miguel had _____ empanadas and then _____."

proficiency. Open sentence starters are more challenging linguistically but can give EBs opportunities to speak in longer sentences. Please refer to activity B.1 in appendix B for more examples of sentence stems.

*Simplify the text.* Textbook problems are often hard to understand. Word problems can be simplified for EBs to provide them access to solve the mathematics. If we do not have time to simplify the text, at times other students can do this for EBs. However, even though the language is simplified, the mathematics should remain challenging.

*Translate key words.* It is *not* effective for students (EBs or non-EBs) to learn key words in an attempt to teach students which operation to use. Some teachers tell students that when they see the word "of" to multiply and the word "less" means to subtract. Apart from not always being true, this robs students of making sense of problems themselves. Yet we can translate key words for EBs—not to reduce their sense making but to provide them access. If some words are translated for EBs in their own language, they may have better understanding of how to solve problems. Refer to table 2.1 for cognates in Spanish and English.

*Word walls.* Similar to translating key words, word walls should be used to provide students access to problems, not to reduce making sense of problems. For example, when learning a lesson on algebra, having technical words on the wall can reinforce our explanations. If EBs are enlightened by a particular lesson, we can reinforce that lesson by taking a picture of our working out and using it as a word wall for future lessons.

Making word walls interactive is even more effective (Ferlazzo and Sypnieski, 2018). Interactive word walls are different from the traditional word walls because the students typically make them and include pictures with labels. By including pictures, the EBs have more access to the content. Ferlazzo and Sypnieski find it effective to pair EBs who speak the same language together and include cognates in the interactive word walls. They

### Textbox 2.7: Problem Before Summarizing

John bought breakfast for two friends and himself. If bagels cost $1.90 and you have to add $.75 for cream cheese, how much would John pay for breakfast if his two friends both wanted a bagel with cream cheese, but John was allergic to cream cheese so he opted out? Also, if John received $4.70 change from a $10 bill, did he receive the correct amount of change? Explain your answer.

caution against having too many interactive word walls in the room at one time as it can become confusing.

*Glossaries and dictionaries.* EBs can make a list of the new math words that they are learning. In addition, they can use and make their own bilingual dictionaries to use as references.

*Technology.* Most students, including EBs, are becoming more engaged with technology because typically it offers multisensory learning. Unfortunately, EBs are less likely to have access to technology. Of course, just playing computer games may not boost EBs' math scores, but strategically using effective technology can motivate EBs to solve problems. Because EBs tend to have less access to computers, attempt to use the computers in school rather than giving homework assignments that require computers.

*Summarizing.* For EBs with limited English proficiency who still struggle to read, we can summarize the problems for them. The goal is to maintain the rigor mathematically but to reduce the linguistic challenge. Imagine EBs with beginning English proficiency attempting the problem in textbox 2.7.

In the advanced stages, the problem in textbox 2.7 may need to only scaffold a little because we want to develop EBs' English proficiency as well as math. However, for other EBs, we could summarize the problem to provide access to the math content. We could change the previous problem by summarizing and making it culturally responsive without reducing the math rigor (textbox 2.8). Notice the sentences are much shorter and in present tense.

With time, we can ask EBs to summarize the problems for us. We can even teach them to change the problem to make it more culturally responsive without altering the mathematics.

*Cooperative learning groups.* This practice not only helps EBs gain access to the math, it can also develop language because group work encourages listening and speaking. However, group work can be ineffective if it is not structured. Sometimes certain students dominate the discourse, so

## *Textbox 2.8: Summarizing a Problem*

Juan buys three tostadas. Tostadas cost $1.90. One apple costs $.75. Juan buys two apples. How much money does Juan spend? Juan pays $10 for these things. What is Juan's change?

teachers may have to intervene to make sure the EBs are participating. Kagan structures are effective because each student in the group is given a role—hence each student can participate. When the students praise the EB for his or her participation, he or she will be more willing to listen to his or her peers.

Another strategy to avoid certain students from dominating the discourse is for teachers to number the pairs or groups and set guidelines, such as: for one minute the ones will talk and the twos will write down what is being solved. Also, in order to have more accountability, the teacher can explain to the class that each member of the group should be able to explain how the problems are solved. This will encourage the groups to make sure each member participates.

One of the most harmful practices is for teachers to ask in whole group discussions for students to raise their hands when they know the answer. EBs, especially at the beginning, need time to process their math work. In order to empathize with EBs and understand how they need time to translate problems in English, solve the following problem in Spanish: "Cinco mas ocho." What might be the steps for you to answer this simple problem?

First you might translate the two numbers to "five" and "eight." You may know that "mas" means more, but you probably wonder what "five more eight" means. You may guess that you have to add, subtract, multiply, or divide. Because five divided by eight would be too challenging, you might discard that option. You may discard the subtraction option too because the word "more" is mentioned. You take a guess and think that the question is asking you to add five and eight. After all that work, you can finally do the math! Thirteen. Then you translate to trece.

Would you be confident enough to raise your hand and share your answer to the whole class? Or would you shut down? Furthermore, look at all of the steps it might take before doing the math. If the teacher were to ask the students to raise their hands when they know the answer, someone not fluent in Spanish would not stand a chance! The Spanish speaker would bypass all of those steps and say "trece" right away.

On the other hand, if the teacher asked you to work in a cooperative group, you would have more access to solve the problems step by step at a slower pace. Working in cooperative groups develops EBs' self-esteem, academic language, and math concepts.

*Chunk it down.* Depending on the EB and his or her English proficiency level, it may be appropriate to teach in small steps. Of course our goal is for each student to gain mastery in all of the topics, but we may get there sooner by taking smaller steps.

*Jigsaw activities.* One advantage of jigsaw activities is that they encourage EBs to develop their English proficiency (chapter 3) as they explain concepts to their classmates. Additionally, jigsaw activities may be helpful for EBs because they only have to worry about being experts in one area of the math problem. If the problem were divided into five parts, they could focus on one part of the problem. For example, instead of focusing on all quadrilaterals, the EBs, and all students, would just be responsible for reporting to their classmates the characteristics of one quadrilateral.

To be sure, we have to have high expectations (chapter 5) for each student, but solving math in another language takes time, and jigsaw activities allow EBs to be experts on a portion of the problem. Eventually, of course, the goal is for EBs to learn all about all of the quadrilaterals, but focusing on one part of a concept can have advantages for some students.

*Acting out problems.* Often EBs struggle to solve word problems because they lack the reading skills in English. However, acting out problems can be an alternative and can allow EBs to visually understand what the problem is asking. Additionally, if the EBs act out problems, they can be successful because the speaking components can be reduced.

*Be flexible and yet have routines.* Being flexible can also allow EBs access to content. There is an erroneous notion that there is only one right way to arrive at an answer in math, but that is not true. Kersaint, Thompson, and Petkova (2009) state that EBs are more likely to have learned to solve math using different algorithms; flexible teachers can allow and praise students for solving problems different ways.

Instead of forcing EBs to use the American algorithm for division, EBs should be encouraged to use their own. Furthermore, many countries focus on decimals more than fractions, so EBs schooled in another country may need to have fractions explained to them.

On the other hand, while we should be flexible, having class routines will facilitate EBs' access because they will know what to expect. If they are not sure how to solve a problem after you provide an explanation, they can be confident that you will allow them opportunities to make sense of the problems with a partner, if that is common practice. EBs will benefit from having routines, especially at the beginning and end of the class. Teachers can end the class offering students opportunities to discuss in pairs or small groups what they learned each day.

## Key Ideas for Providing Access

- Did you try to solve the problems in figure 2.1? Not only do EBs have the challenge of solving math in English, they also may be accustomed to using different math symbols.
- If EBs are going to be successful at solving math problems, you will need to provide them with access to the math.
- Many teachers attempt to adapt lesson plans after they have been made. It is better to take EBs into consideration while you are planning than to try to adapt plans after the lessons are already made.
- It is beneficial to meet with EBs before the math lesson to preteach vocabulary words and background knowledge.
- We should consider how we speak to EBs—remember GRASSES (gestures; repeat; avoid idioms, puns, and jokes; speak slowly; simple sentences; expressive; and smile.
- There are numerous scaffolding techniques to provide our students with access to solve the math content. Using visuals and scaffolding the language are key components of many of the strategies.
- Please refer to activity G.1 in appendix G for a self-assessment of the key ideas in this chapter.

∽

# CHAPTER THREE

# Developing Language

My first year of teaching was at a school with 99% Spanish-speaking EBs. I had high expectations for each of my students. I used more visuals and hands-on activities. I connected vocabulary with their Spanish and always had more than one way to explain a strategy or tool. I put my students into groups and gave them many opportunities for discussions. These strategies work for all students labeled EBs or not.

My second year I had three students in my class with zero English-speaking skills. They were very shy and did not seem interested in participating. They seemed to feel inferior because they didn't speak English. My goal was to boost their confidence. I used the same strategies as I did my first year. After a month, they were like the other students—walking around with confidence, asking questions and engaging in the learning.

—Shelby, third-grade teacher from Dallas, Texas

## What Is Developing Language?

The paradox is that not only should we provide each of our students access to solve problems but we also need to develop their language. Many teachers understand that they need to provide access for EBs to solve content, but they often forget about the importance of developing EBs' language. Many teachers who instruct math consider this to be the role of the English Language Arts (ELA) teacher (sometimes it is the same teacher) or ESL teachers. We must develop the language of all our students, including EBs in all subjects, including mathematics so they can successfully solve word problems.

The third Mathematical Practice from the Common Core State Standards calls for students to develop arguments and critique each other's arguments. For non–Common Core states, such as Texas, the process standards also require students to develop mathematical arguments and reason about math. This requires students to have mathematical language and academic language.

In traditional math classes there tends to be little discussion on how to solve problems—the focus is more on getting the correct answer. However, today, regardless of whether you are in a Common Core state, there is more emphasis on students explaining how they solve the problems. For EBs to be successful justifying their answers, we need to develop their language.

## Developing Spanish-Speaking EBs' Language

By developing EBs' language we need to consider their math language, English proficiency, and Spanish proficiency.

For the purpose of this book, math language refers to the technical vocabulary words needed to solve math problems. The words used in math can be dense and hard to understand. Furthermore, because there are plenty of words that have special meanings, it can be challenging (Zwiers, 2008). Words such as "balance," "table," and "odd" mean something else outside of math class. Furthermore, mathematics is more sequential than other subjects, so if a student lacks mastery of prior knowledge due to vocabulary challenges, it will be harder to acquire new concepts.

Because it is impossible to solve math problems without knowing these technical words, teachers usually do take time to explain these words to both non-EBs and EBs. Fortunately, lots of the math terms are similar in the two languages. Refer to the list of cognates (words similar in Spanish and English) in table 2.1.

Surprisingly, the easier tier 2 words can be more of a challenge for EBs than tier 3 (technical) words. EBs tend to learn the basic words (tier 1) on the playground and in the cafeteria. However, tier 2 words are not being taught in class because most of the non-EBs already know these words. Words such as "amount," "show your work," and "closest" are examples of tier 2 words; they are seldom heard in EBs' social settings and are skipped over in class. Furthermore, these words are not usually cognates and they lack context.

For example, if Spanish-speaking EBs were asked to find the hypotenuse of the triangle formed when a ladder touches a roof, they may understand a technical word like "hypotenuse" because it is similar in Spanish and the teacher explained the word, but they struggle to understand the other words. Without knowing the meaning of "ladder," "touches," or "roof," it can be frustrating. We often tell non-EBs not to select a book if there are more than five words on a page that they don't understand. Now imagine how EBs may feel if they do not understand five words or more in one math problem.

Thus, mainstream teachers are responsible for teaching English as well as math so EBs learn tier 2 words. Years ago it was common practice to send students to ESL classes until they had a command of English. Today we know that it takes more than five years for EBs to acquire academic English (Cummins, 1981). Sometimes EBs are placed into mainstream classes, according to Cummins, after acquiring a degree of oral fluency without acquiring academic language. In order to be successful in the classroom, EBs will need to know academic language, including tier 2 words.

Most teachers are aware that they need to provide EBs access to the content, but in their attempt to do so, they often provide too much linguistic scaffolding. Giving EBs work with few words will not develop their language. Apart from providing our students access to the content, there is also a need to develop their math language and academic language so they can be successful at solving math problems in the future (de Jong and Harper, 2011; Ewing, Gresham, and Dickey, 2019). Thus, EBs need to be challenged mathematically as well as linguistically.

Too often teachers focus purely on developing EBs' English proficiency and ignore their Spanish proficiency. By offering EBs opportunities to occasionally solve math in Spanish, they will develop academic Spanish, and this can be transferred to learning academic English. Milner (2015) reports how he visited a school where the non-EBs were learning Spanish. The person that showed him around was so happy that the non-EBs would be learning Spanish and other languages. This would make non-EBs bilingual and even trilingual.

However, as Milner points out, the EBs were not offered the same privilege—they were only taught English and their first language was ignored in school. Milner argues for schools to meet the needs of each student. When non-EBs learn Spanish, they do not forget about their English, so why should we ignore the Spanish-speaking EBs' first language?

It may be overwhelming for teachers who do not speak Spanish fluently to develop students' academic Spanish language. However, regardless of our

Spanish fluency, we can encourage our students to learn Spanish. Supporting our students in speaking Spanish will also promote their English proficiency. Thus, we should give EBs opportunities to listen, speak, read, and write in their own language. Following are more strategies for developing EBs' math language and English and Spanish proficiency. They are divided into speaking and listening, reading, and writing.

## Speaking and Listening

Lots of classes follow a pattern referred to as "Initiation, Response, and Evaluate" (IRE). With this pattern, the teacher typically begins the conversation and asks the class a question in whole group discussion. One of the students with a lot of confidence raises his or her hand and answers. Then the teacher evaluates if that student has given the response she was looking for. If not, the teacher may call on another confident student to respond until she is given the correct answer.

To imagine how frustrated the students may become when discourse is not shared, imagine the following game. A teacher gives a racket to each of two students and begins playing with them. She initiates the play and passes the ball to one of the students. The student returns the ball to the teacher, and the teacher sends it to the second student. The other students watch as the teacher continues passing the ball to one or another of these same two students, ignoring the rest of the class.

Most teachers would agree that it would be unfair for a few students to play a game while the others watch. Likewise, each student should be involved in discourse. Furthermore, there should be opportunities for student-student discourse. The IRE approach is not effective for developing EBs' language—they are merely listening to a few students and the teacher. Just as teachers write math objectives for lessons because they want to make sure concepts are learned, they can also write language objectives to make sure students have opportunities to speak in each class (Borgioli, 2008).

Instead of the teacher dominating the discourse, we need to give students opportunities to talk and justify their answers. If we ask more questions and do less telling, students will learn math concepts more deeply and will develop their language (Ewing, Gresham, and Dickey, 2019). Teachers should make an effort to engage each student, according to Coggins (2014), and refrain from allowing some students to dominate the discourse. If students are allowed time to discuss in pairs, this will present opportunities for everyone to participate.

Hufferd-Ackles, Fuson, and Sherin (2004) trained four teachers to shift the discourse from the teachers to the predominately Spanish-speaking students by teaching inquiry-based lessons. With the advice of the researchers, the teachers asked students to justify the answers to their problems. They suggested that the teachers use visual aids and encourage their students to draw pictures and give explanations when they solved their problems.

The authors found that by the end of the year the students in the class studied were speaking for longer periods of time and asking more questions. Although it can be challenging for EBs with limited English proficiency to speak, they will benefit from classrooms like this one where the students have countless opportunities to talk.

In the vignette written by Shelby at the beginning of the chapter, she offered her students lots of opportunities to speak in small groups. Shelby provided her students access by using lots of visuals and taught her EBs Spanish/English cognates. Like other EBs who are not proficient at English and are placed in a monolingual setting, her students went through a silent phase. However, by having high expectations for them, putting them in small groups, and boosting their trust, these students integrated well and became active members of the class.

Teachers can adapt their expectations for EBs according to their proficiency (Bresser, Melanese, and Sphar, 2009). For those students who are at the beginning stages of learning English, we can ask them yes/no questions, but as they become more efficient, we need to ask questions that encourage them to answer in full sentences. If teachers or peers know some Spanish vocabulary, this can help EBs immensely—not only does it help EBs have access to the content, but when the teacher attempts to learn the EBs' first language, the students feel valued.

There is a misconception that if EBs are speaking their own language, it impedes them from learning English. In fact, literature shows that EBs who have a strong foundation in their own language will learn English faster (Cummins, 1981). Thus, we should give Spanish-speaking EBs opportunities to discuss problems in their own language.

Following are strategies for listening and speaking—most that promote listening also promote speaking, so they are listed together.

*Teach EBs how to justify their answers.* We are often taught not to argue, but developing mathematical arguments is one of the standards for most states. Learning how to form mathematical arguments and critiquing the arguments of others takes time, especially in a second language. We can't just tell students to discuss whether one-third is bigger than one-fourth. We will need to model the process, emphasizing that it is the argument of our peers that we are critiquing, not the person who presents the argument. The whole process may be new for EBs.

We can make sentence stems to help them justify their answers and carry on their part of the dialogue. For example, "I like what _____ said about _____, but I think he may have forgotten about _____. He could have included _____."

*Teach students oracy.* Mary, a first-grade teacher from Ithaca, New York, put her students in small groups but noticed that her students could not understand each other because they were mumbling and not enunciating. Now she gives them classes in oracy. She models how students should speak and gives them plenty of opportunities to speak in pairs. Mary purposefully teaches students to make eye contact and listen to one another.

It is not enough to just put EBs in small groups and ask them to explain math concepts; they need to be intentionally taught how to develop mathematical arguments. While students will not learn how to speak effectively if they are in rows and the teacher does all of the talking, there is more to be done than simply putting students in groups and asking them to talk. We shouldn't assume that students come to school with proper listening and speaking skills. We can teach students to face the speaker, maintain eye contact, and refrain from interrupting. We can model how to enunciate and speak loud enough for the other students to hear.

If two or more students in the class speak Spanish, we can observe their oracy skills when they speak in their first language. It may be easier for students to maintain eye contact, enunciate, and use proper tone and volume if we allow them to discuss math in Spanish. With time, we can make the transfer of applying all these skills when they speak in English.

*Respect the silent period.* It is typical for EBs to go through a silent period for about six weeks when they first begin learning English. This is normal development and should be respected. Just because EBs do not talk does not mean they are not learning English—they are learning. It is important for us to build trust with students during this phase. Thus, we can avoid calling on EBs to share to the whole class because this can be embarrassing. However, as the trust level builds, we can ask EBs yes/no questions that require them to nod their heads instead of speaking.

When students are moving out of the silent period, it is important to avoid overcorrecting their English and to let them know that they are in a safe environment where it is okay to make mistakes. At this stage, although the students will not speak much, they need to be in a language-rich classroom that gives them ample opportunities to listen. As they become more comfortable, they will share their math strategies with us and with other peers. It is imperative that EBs feel safe and accepted so that they will risk sharing their mathematical arguments.

*Praise EBs for sharing.* Can you imagine justifying a math problem in Spanish? Sharing can be very intimidating and yet so important for EBs' growth. Instead of overcorrecting their English grammar, we can praise them for taking the risk to share. If we do, they will share more often and develop their language.

*Share the discourse.* Teachers tend to speak too much. We learn by practicing and we can't expect EBs to learn to speak English if we do not give them lots and lots of practice. Some teachers wrongly conclude that the EBs are learning English from them. The truth is, if teachers are lecturing too much, the EBs shut down in class and for the most part must learn to speak at recess and in the cafeteria.

*Consider EBs' English proficiency.* Bresser, Melanese, and Sphar (2009) maintain that if EBs struggle to justify their answers, then teachers should facilitate their success by asking questions to EBs that require minimal discourse. Teachers can ask yes/no questions at the beginning. Even when EBs possess limited English proficiency, we can still encourage them to develop mathematical arguments. With the aid of manipulatives, EBs can justify their mathematical reasoning, albeit with grammar mistakes.

As EBs become more fluent, we can ask more open questions that require them to justify their answers in more depth. Assessing EBs' English proficiency will help us make appropriate decisions to facilitate their participation.

*Circle time.* Students can be taught to get together in a circle and talk one at a time about math concepts. If one of their peers is talking, they wait their turn. If necessary, they raise their thumb to be called on. Before having whole group discussions, the teacher allows her students time to share in pairs so that even if EBs don't get the opportunity to share with the whole class, at least they have had an opportunity to speak and listen to a classmate. Being in a circle develops math language more than a typical class arrangement because each student has opportunities to share.

*Morning meetings.* Similar to circle time, having morning meetings can be used simply to create class community; math activities can also be done. In this way, EBs understand that math can be fun. Later, during the math class, the teacher can connect the learning in the math class with the math done during the meeting. Morning meetings offer EBs opportunities to develop listening and speaking skills in a nonthreatening way. Refer to textbox 3.1 for a game that promotes geometry skills, develops language, and creates class community.

*Storytelling.* Storytelling was already mentioned in chapter 1 because it develops students' positive math mindset. They tend to enjoy storytelling— it is more personal and more emotional than typical teacher and student

## Textbox 3.1: Morning Meeting Game

### Human Transportador (Protractor)

Always facing the center of the circle, students move to one of four points in the circle (0, 90, 180, or 270). The teacher says that she is going to her right or left and mentions how many degrees she will go. For example, if she is at 90 degrees and turns left 90 degrees, she will end up at point 180. When she goes to the group at that point, she can shake everyone's hand. When students learn the four points, more points, such as 45, 135, 225, and 315 degrees, can be added.

An extension is an elimination game. The teacher or leader closes her eyes and the students quietly move to one of the four points. The leader randomly calls out one of the points. The numbers can be called out in Spanish. If the students' point is called, they have to sit down. Then the students move to another point of their choice, and the leader keeps calling until there is only one student left.

Sentence stems should be displayed for games and morning meetings. Appropriate sentence stems for "Class Transportador" might be: The leader moves to the _____ (right or left) _____ (0, 90, 180, 270) degrees.

explanations. Because it is so enjoyable, storytelling is an excellent opportunity to hook students and connect them to the math content while developing their language at the same time. After you model storytelling, students can tell stories to their peers at the beginning of math lessons.

Storytelling is common in Latin countries. In Mexico, Calaveras are short stories or poems that are told on Día del los Muertos (The Day of the Dead). Perhaps you could allow a student to read Calaveras in Spanish and tie them to the math lesson.

*Use puppets.* EBs who are self-conscious about making mistakes when they speak may open up with puppets. Puppets can be used for many purposes—before the lesson to discuss background knowledge about a topic, explaining how to solve a problem, or to summarize what they learned in the math lesson. For more engagement, students could make their own puppets.

*Play games.* There are many math games that promote listening and speaking as well as promoting mathematical concepts. One game in Mexico called

"Lotería" is similar to Bingo. This game is very popular and many Mexicans living in the United States still play it. Some ESL classes use this game to develop students' vocabularies. The game consists of boards with pictures such as the melon, pear, and umbrella. One person randomly calls out shapes and the other players try to fill up their boards by putting a counter, often frijoles, for each corresponding picture.

After playing Lotería, the teacher can make math problems related to the shapes. The Mexican EB will be motivated to solve the problems that are related to a popular game in their culture. Also, after playing Lotería, we can tell the EBs that we are going to play "Math Lotería" and play Multiplication Bingo. By allowing the EBs to play Lotería first, they can easily make the transition to play Multiplication Bingo.

*Pair/share.* If teachers dominate the discourse, students stop listening. Sharing math concepts can be an excellent opportunity for students to develop their math language and get motivated to learn. Pair/share can be implemented at the beginning of the lesson to pique students' interests, during the lesson to promote reasoning, and at the end of the lesson for students to consolidate mathematical concepts.

At times, EBs can be with other EBs, and at times they can be paired with non-EBs. At first non-EBs may not know how to communicate with EBs, but we can teach them to use multiple visuals and gestures when they communicate with all students, including EBs.

As previously mentioned, we should avoid asking the students in whole group discussions to raise their hands when they know their answers. At the beginning stages, EBs will need time to translate problems from English to Spanish and back to English. This process takes time and EBs will rarely translate fast enough to raise their hands in time to answer the question. Without having practice to speak, our EBs are not developing their English proficiency.

Our goal might be to have our EBs share with the whole class. This may boost their confidence and even social status. Before having whole group discussions, we should first have students work in pairs or groups. When EBs share, we should listen in so we can ask questions to encourage them to delve deeper into the content. EBs are more likely to take the chance of sharing with the whole class if we first validate that they have a strong mathematical argument for this. If the EB does not want to share with the whole group, the teacher can reduce the risk by asking the EB if he or she wants to share with the help of a partner.

If EBs still do not want to share, we can ask EBs if we can revoice their reasoning to the whole class. Often the students who share are the ones who get validated by the teacher, but we can also validate students by revoicing their ideas. For example, the teacher could say, "Marta says that one-fourth is less than one-third. Discuss in pairs why Marta is correct." This sends the message that we value the students' mathematical thinking. Even if the students opt not to share with the whole class, at least they have had opportunities to solve problems with a partner.

*Summarization.* This skill is one of the most effective practices for all students (Frey, Hattie, and Fisher, 2018). Students retain concepts better when they have opportunities to review concepts in their own words. The bonus is that EBs have the added goal of developing their speaking and listening skills when they are asked to summarize what they have learned with a partner.

*Sentence starters or stems.* As mentioned previously, sentence starters give EBs opportunities both to better understand their peers and to speak. Sentence starters can aid EBs in sharing in discussions about math.

*Record conversations.* It may be helpful to record EBs' conversations while they are discussing math concepts; typically this should not be done until they have had ample practice speaking. At this point, they can be motivated to discuss concepts in detail and then as a final product explain the concepts in detail on tape. Later other students can listen to the audiotapes.

*Prompts.* Writing prompts are common in the classroom, but these can also be used to generate discussions. For example, teachers could give a prompt to students to summarize what they liked about the math lesson or to debate a point. Note that prompts should be written and be accessible for EBs with limited English proficiency.

*Stations.* Too often math classes are taught as a whole group, which can make EBs in particular feel alienated. Being in small groups is less intimidating and offers students more opportunities to talk. Setting up math in stations allows students to learn the math concepts and develop their language at the same time.

*Total physical response (TPR).* This practice has a high kinesthetic component and is typically used for developing EBs' vocabulary. Typically the teacher will ask the student to do certain actions and the EBs develop their vocabulary as they act out the short commands. When students do the actions, it increases memory retention. Simon Says is an example of TPR. This technique can be applied to math. For example, the teacher could say, "Simon says make a triangle with your fingers." Textbox 3.2 is an activity based on TPR for math.

Frequently TPR is used to improve students' listening vocabulary. Students can look at the teacher and guess what the words mean by focusing on the teacher's actions. In textbox 3.2, students have opportunities to speak as

## Textbox 3.2: A Total Physical Response Activity

Make a triangle with your fingers. Now make the triangle obtuse. Explain to your neighbor why your triangle is obtuse. Now make it isosceles. How about an equilateral triangle? Can you make a hexagon with your fingers? Can you make a hexagon with your partner's fingers and your fingers?

they justify their thinking. If students struggle with the English vocabulary, they can still use their fingers for their mathematical argument.

*Reciprocal teaching.* This approach is more common in reading but can be a strong motivator to get EBs speaking and talking about math. Reciprocal teaching is based on the premise that the students are the teachers. EBs listen carefully to their peers because they know that they too will have the opportunity to teach. There are variations of reciprocal teaching, but there are typically four parts: predict, clarify, solve, and summarize.

One of the most effective ways to get EBs to participate is by assigning each student a role. The predictors, with the help of the group, guess what the operation of the math problem might be. The clarifier makes sure everyone in the group understands the vocabulary words and discusses the steps necessary for solving the problem.

As the group solves the problem, the solver explains the steps out loud to the group. Last, the summarizer reflects on the process and how the group could refine the process in the future to do even better. Reciprocal teaching has plenty of opportunities for students to speak and listen. In order to facilitate EBs' access to the problems, the teacher or other students in the group can make sentence stems. Refer to tables C.1 and C.2 in appendix C for more examples of reciprocal teaching.

### Reading

Reading math problems in English can be especially challenging for some EBs—not only are they required to solve problems in a second language, they may not even have experience solving word problems in their first language. (In some Latin countries, there is more emphasis on arithmetic and less on solving word problems.) However, even though reading in a second language may be challenging, EBs must be given ample practice in reading and solving problems within their zone of proximal development.

*Preteach.* As mentioned in the previous chapter, we can preteach vocabulary words to provide EBs access to math problems. We should also activate EBs' prior knowledge of the math problems and have a discussion. Modeling how to read problems out loud can encourage EBs in reading out loud too. Preteaching is more proactive than remediation. While we want to challenge our students, predicting what students may need in advance and preteaching necessary vocabulary keeps learning productive rather than waiting until they "fail" and then offering remediation.

*Draw problems.* Solving longer problems and multistep problems in English can be overwhelming for EBs. However, by drawing the problems students can be taught to read and make sense of problems step by step.

*Work with a partner.* If EBs work with a partner, it can boost their confidence. They can work with non-EBs in English and at times work with another EB translating and explaining the significance of the problem in Spanish. Of course, working with a partner can help EBs read as well as developing their listening and speaking skills.

*Incorporate games.* Reading math problems is challenging for all students, especially students reading in a second language. EBs can be motivated to read by playing nonthreatening games. Students can play computer games individually or in pairs. EBs will be motivated to read the math problems so they can continue to play the games.

*Give EBs ample practice solving word problems.* According to Garrison, Ponce, and Amaral (2007), word problems, although challenging, are imperative for EBs. Teachers may be tempted to give computational problems without language to make it easier for EBs to participate, but this would not help EBs develop their reading proficiency in English.

Use the present tense, high-frequency words, and short sentences for EBs with limited English proficiency. As the year progresses, more challenging words and longer sentences should be used. Solving word problems, although challenging, is another opportunity to develop EBs' language.

*Be active.* We want EBs to be active rather than simply staring at the problems. Encourage students to put question marks by the parts that they don't understand and to check the parts that they might comprehend. EBs can also be taught to underline or paraphrase the question and cross out parts of the problem that are not related to the question. Last, EBs can be asked to write out the parts that they don't understand and the parts that they do understand. This leads us to the last section for developing language in math class.

## Writing

Writing about math can be an excellent opportunity for EBs to consolidate mathematical reasoning and develop their language at the same time. Often we focus on procedural knowledge and simply ask students to memorize names. This is lower-level learning. Alternatively, we can have students write and explain conceptual knowledge and focus on deeper learning. The bonus is that when we ask our EBs to write we can analyze their mathematical reasoning. Following are some strategies to make the writing easier.

*Allow pictures and sketches.* It may be easier for EBs, especially at the beginning stages, to include pictures with their writing. For example, teachers may not understand EBs' definition of a nonregular octagon, but by looking at a sketch of the shape, teachers can evaluate EBs' mathematical understanding of the content.

*Write in pairs or small groups.* Allowing students to write in groups develops not only writing skills but also listening and speaking skills. It may be intimidating for EBs to write by themselves, but they will have a sense of accomplishment if their group writes a final product.

*Math journal.* Students should be encouraged to keep math journals to jot down ideas. Teachers can ask affective questions about how difficult the math lesson was for students or ask conceptual questions. Open questions will encourage students to write more. EBs should be allowed to occasionally write in Spanish. Journals do not have to be graded, but teachers should collect and read them to get feedback about EBs' academic language fluency, affect, and conceptual understanding.

In order to facilitate EBs' access to writing, which can be overwhelming, teachers should encourage EBs to write in Spanish if they do not know the word in English. Another option to get EBs writing is to encourage them to draw pictures with their mathematical explanations.

*Write math problems.* EBs will have more access to solving problems if they are related to their personal lives. It takes teachers time to write relevant problems, but if EBs are given opportunities to write their own problems, they can enhance their fluency and solve word problems that are relevant.

*Teach writing strategies.* It can be overwhelming for EBs to write because they might be afraid of making mistakes. However, being told that they can prewrite at the beginning and not worry about grammar and spelling may reduce the stress and allow students to focus on jotting down their ideas. Allow students to include words in their own language, and then they can find the translation in the revising stage.

*Computers.* If possible, EBs can be encouraged to write on the computers. Not only do they have access to translate vocabulary with the use of computers, but they can also learn to use word processors so they can focus more on the content and less on grammar.

## Key Ideas for Developing Language

- EBs need to have access to content, but they also need their language developed in all classes, including math class, so they can solve math problems on their own.
- EBs will not develop their language unless they have ample opportunities to listen, speak, read, and write.
- Apart from putting students in groups, teachers need to teach EBs how to develop mathematical arguments and critique the arguments of their peers.
- Teachers usually teach technical math words, but EBs often struggle with tier 2 words that non-EBs commonly know. EBs don't hear these words in the playground or cafeteria and they are not taught them in class.
- Most EBs go through a silent period, and this should be respected. If EBs are stimulated by listening to many conversations, they will open up and speak when they are ready.
- EBs will take the chance to share their ideas if they feel safe and accepted.
- We need to consider EBs' level of English proficiency when we ask them questions. At the beginning stages we can ask yes/no questions, but later we can push them by asking open questions that require longer answers.
- Reading and writing can be challenging for EBs, but with lots of opportunities for practice, they can improve.
- Please refer to activity G.1 in appendix G for a self-assessment of the key ideas in this chapter.

~

# CHAPTER FOUR

# Productive Struggle

My class is entirely made of EBs. In fact, four of my students speak mostly Spanish and are just learning to say a few phrases in English. I noticed that when I put my students in groups, the students who were more proficient in English and confident in math would dominate the conversations. The others would just watch. I wanted each of my students to be challenged.

Now, I give the students roles. I typically give the role of facilitator to my GT students and the role of my reporter to my tier 2 and 3 students. The facilitator's role is to ask questions while the other students explain.

—Ben, a fifth-grade teacher from Elgin, Texas

## What Is Productive Struggle?

In some countries, like Japan, teachers allow students a long time to solve problems, but American teachers jump in too soon to help students, especially in math (Hiebert and Grouws, 2007). We used to try to plan how to make math easy for students, but now we should plan on how to get our students to struggle (Seeley, 2015). Struggling is good. Students learn mathematics with deeper meaning when they grapple to make sense of problems within their zone of proximal development (Dixon, Adams, and Nolan, 2015; Hiebert and Grouws, 2007; Vygotsky, 1978). This is called productive struggle.

After attending a professional development on productive struggle, a middle school math teacher named Shanan, who teaches in a rural school in Texas, has changed her approach to teaching math. She used to figure out strategies for making math easier for her students. Now she plans how to engage her students in productive struggle. Shanan looks for open, challenging tasks to engage her students. Instead of telling her students how to solve problems, she asks probing questions and allows them opportunities to make sense of the problems.

With this new approach, Shanan has noticed a change in the students' mindsets. She says, "From the highest to the lowest, they love to 'struggle' in math class. Students walk in asking, 'Are we doing a struggle today?'"

Another example of students engaging in productive struggle is at the Japanese School in Greenwich, Connecticut. Once a year the school has an open house and invites educators to visit and observe. The school instruction is completely in Japanese; even if you don't understand the words, you will be impressed at how happy and hard working the students are. The students genuinely enjoy being challenged.

For example, how were you taught to multiply two digits by two digits? In third or fourth grade your teacher probably reviewed previous knowledge, which was multiplying two digits by one digit, and then *she* demonstrated how to multiply the new way. Next she would pass out a worksheet and ask you to practice. The problem with this approach is that it is not challenging and it stifles creativity; there is too much focus on solving the problem using the teacher's method. We tend to spoon feed students and reduce the challenge by telling students how to solve problems.

Teachers at the Japanese School have a different approach. The teacher frames the problem for the students and asks them to discover how *they* might multiply two digits by two digits. The emphasis is not on getting the right answer but on developing as many strategies as possible to solve the problem.

It is fascinating to watch how long the students persevere at solving one problem. In lots of other schools, the students stop working when the first student raises his or her hand and says, "What do I do when I am finished?" After that interruption it is difficult to get the rest of the class back on target. The students at the Japanese School are different. They work on one problem until they have solved it, at which point they try to solve it again using a different strategy.

After twenty minutes of problem solving, the teacher asks the students to share their strategies. The students are enthralled to know how their classmates solve the same problem. Students applaud their peers after they explain the solutions and give extra loud applause for a peer who thinks out of the box. Students experience the joy of the light bulb effect. They struggle and struggle with a solution and finally feel the satisfaction of victory after discovering effective solutions. We want all of our students, including Spanish-speaking EBs, to experience productive struggle.

## Engaging Spanish-Speaking EBs in Productive Struggle

Ben, mentioned in the vignette at the beginning of the chapter, explains that some of his students were dominating the conversations when working in groups. While it can be beneficial for EBs to work in small groups, he still noticed that some students were solving and explaining the problems while the others merely watched. In order to engage each of his students in productive struggle, he assigned his students roles. By being proactive, Ben ensures that each of his students engage in productive struggle.

An example of teachers engaging in productive struggle in a second language occurred at a National Council of Teachers of Mathematics conference in Philadelphia in 2012. Even though none of the participants spoke Vietnamese, the instructor of one session taught a math lesson in his native language. At first the teachers were ready to give up when they heard the instructor speaking Vietnamese, but he smiled and encouraged the teachers to continue to solve the math problem.

The instructor provided the teachers access by using visuals and giving them manipulatives. Another strategy he used was allowing the teachers to work in pairs before explaining their justifications to the whole group. Obviously, the teachers' vocabulary in Vietnamese was limited, but with the instructor's support and the use of manipulatives, the teachers managed to develop a mathematical argument and persevered to solve a challenging problem.

It is hard to engage in productive struggle in mathematics when lacking proficiency in the language of instruction, but the leader facilitated the teachers. He had high expectations for his teachers, he created a caring atmosphere, he asked lots of questions, and he allowed the teachers ample time to process. If we use these steps, we can engage our EBs in productive struggle—each and every one of them.

Unfortunately, many have low expectations for EBs in math. When one preservice teacher described how she would teach math to EBs, she replied that she would give them less work (Ewing, 2016). This preservice teacher was not referring to any student in particular, but she had acquired the belief that EBs in general should be given less math work. The National Council of

Teachers of Mathematics (2014) states that too often teachers fail to engage certain groups of students in productive struggle.

If teachers believe that EBs will not be successful, this can be a self-fulfilling prophecy. Larson et al. (2012) add that the goal for teachers should not be to treat all students the same but for teachers to look for ways to challenge all students. Where do we develop beliefs that certain students are not as good at math as others? It is important for us to examine our expectations for EBs and provide them access instead of spoon feeding them.

Teachers who have low expectations for students also tend to provide less time for those students to make sense of problems and persevere to solve them (Kilpatrick, Swafford, and Findell, 2001). It may take EBs more time to solve problems because they may be solving the problems in Spanish, but we need to give them the time and keep our expectations high. After all, EBs may have more resiliency than non-EBs—they experience solving problems in a second language on a daily basis. That takes resiliency! We should focus on EBs' assets, such as the fact that they are learning at least two languages.

Instead of giving EBs less or easy math, we need to accommodate their needs so they can engage in rigorous math. Murrey (2008) concludes that teachers may provide access to EBs with the use of gestures, drawings, and manipulatives (chapter 2), but they must be sure that the math is still challenging. Some teachers assign EBs worksheets that do not challenge them. This may serve to keep the EBs busy and perhaps quiet, but of course our goal should be to challenge each of our students mathematically and linguistically.

By giving EBs challenging tasks, we are also developing their English proficiency. As discussed earlier, when the students at the Japanese School were given challenging problems, they were anxious to share their answers with their peers. If EBs are given boring worksheets, they probably will not be motivated to share their solutions with their peers, but if they are challenged and finally solve a problem, it is only natural that they will want to share the process. When EBs discuss challenging problems, they develop their English proficiency and mathematical concepts.

Most teachers will say that they give all of their students challenging work, but some teachers have a discrepancy between their beliefs and actual practices (Celedon-Pattichis and Ramirez, 2012). The researchers interviewed teachers who thought that they were meeting every students' needs, but when the teachers examined their practices on video, they realized that they did not ask EBs enough challenging questions to engage them in productive struggle. We can all benefit from examining our practices to make sure we are challenging all of our students.

Zahner (2012) observed a bilingual teacher who facilitated students' access to algebra by asking questions in two languages. He found that having high expectations, being caring, asking questions, and allowing students ample time to solve problems helped students solve challenging problems. Zahner (2012) posits that even monolingual teachers could engage EBs to solve challenging problems by offering a supportive environment and opportunities to talk about mathematics in their own language. This is a reminder that each teacher can engage each student in productive struggle.

Following are strategies to facilitate EBs to engage in productive struggle. The strategies are divided into four parts: having high expectations, creating a caring classroom, asking questions, and allowing students ample time to solve problems.

## High Expectations

On average, our Spanish-speaking EBs are not doing well in math—not because they are incapable but because we are not trained to meet their needs. If we have high expectations for EBs and provide them access, they can engage in rigorous mathematics.

*Assume competence.* EBs are capable of engaging in high-level math. After all, they have already engaged in challenging tasks by learning a second language. Instead of thinking of EBs as "less" because they are not fluent in English, we can recognize them for being language experts. When we acknowledge our EBs for their language expertise, this confidence will transfer to math and other subjects as well.

*Appreciate EBs' resiliency.* There is a big drive in education today to push students to be resilient and not give up. EBs are excellent examples of resilient students—they solve math in a second language. We must not take this for granted, and we should share with non-EBs how resilient EBs are for solving math in a second language. Non-EBs should hear us praise EBs for their resiliency.

*Teach positivity.* If our EBs are positive, they are more likely to persevere to solve rigorous math problems. If we model positivity, our students will be positive as well. Being optimistic and having high expectations for EBs can be self-fulfilling. Eric Jensen, an expert in giving workshops for teachers, starts each day by asking participants what they appreciate today. Let's ask our EBs what they appreciate. It is impossible to focus on appreciation and have a negative emotion at the same time. Textbox 4.1 is a guide for how teachers can get students to begin their day or period on a positive note.

The short activity in textbox 4.1 puts students in a positive state, ready to solve challenging math problems. Moving around, listening to music, talking

> ### *Textbox 4.1: Students Discuss What They Appreciate*
>
> - Teacher says, "Please stand up and when you hear the music touch five chairs."
> - Teacher puts on music that the students like for thirty seconds.
> - Teacher says, "Find a partner and answer the two questions on the monitor."
> - In pairs, students answer the two questions. One question can be what they appreciate today and the other question can be a review question.
> - Teacher says, "Tell your partner you enjoyed working with her/him."

to a classmate, focusing on what they appreciate, and reviewing background knowledge will prepare students to engage in productive struggle. The added bonus is that the EBs are developing their English by listening to short directions from the teacher and discussing with a partner.

Brain research supports the importance of being positive and of facilitating our students to move. Eric Jensen (2019) explains how neurotransmitters can boost student learning. We can increase our students' level of dopamine by having fun activities and encouraging movement. Higher dopamine levels help students focus and even try harder. Making your students feel safe in class can boost serotonin levels—high serotonin improves memory skills. In short, by being positive our EBs will be more likely to engage in productive struggle.

*Do not overdo mathematical scaffolding.* Some teachers scaffold when it is not necessary. A common strategy is "I do, we do, you do." This can occasionally be effective for EBs who struggle with a lack of access to the content, but if this is overdone, EBs are robbed of making sense of problems themselves. If the teacher solves similar problems, then the students are robbed of making sense of problems on their own.

*Choose challenging tasks.* Even though EBs may need some scaffolding to help them have access to the content, we need to keep the mathematics challenging. Tasks should be within their zone, not below.

*Push EBs.* Students will often work up to our expectations. If we nudge them, then they will realize that we have high expectations for them and will work accordingly. We should challenge EBs in improving both their mathematical skills and their English proficiency skills.

*Set goals.* Teachers should set meaningful mathematical goals for their students and encourage their EBs to set goals too. Setting clear and measurable goals enables students to work hard to achieve them. When students work hard and finally achieve their goals, they experience a special feeling called eudemonic happiness. This happiness is more fulfilling than the temporary hedonic happiness that is achieved from video games and watching TV (Jensen, 2019). Thus, if students persevere to solve challenging math problems and achieve their goals and are rewarded with eudemonic happiness, this cycle will continue.

If EBs set goals that are related to their culture and/or families, these will be more meaningful. For example, they might say that they are going to pass that math test so they can be the first one in their family to go to college. Of course, it will not be the same if the teacher sets that goal for the students—it needs to come from them. When students set meaningful math goals, it will positively addict them.

*Focus on the math.* While we need to develop EBs' English proficiency, if we overcorrect their English grammar, they will become frustrated and not persevere to solve problems. If EBs are in a safe environment, they can develop sophisticated mathematical arguments, albeit with grammatical errors. Sometimes students lose the rich mathematical ideas that EBs have because they lack the English proficiency to explain their ideas, but the teacher or a classmate can revoice their thinking.

*Foster mathematical identities through names.* By referring to our students as "matemáticos" (mathematicians) we can motivate our EBs to engage in challenging math. This approach is effective because it deals with students' identity. If we call our students mathematicians, it relays the message that they belong in the mathematical community, and saying it in Spanish recognizes their language and culture. We want our students to believe that they are mathematicians and thus act like other mathematicians who engage in productive struggle.

We can also call our students "los mayas" (Mayans), "los aztecas" (Aztecs), or "los incas" (Incans) in math class. The Mayans were strong astronomers and as a result developed an efficient number system for measurement. Famous for the solar calendars, the Aztecs were precise mathematicians. The Incas also used a calendar and, like us today, divided their year into twelve months.

Reviewing a little history with students and then calling them Mayans, Aztecs, and Incans in Spanish is a great way to foster their mathematical identities because it has the potential to tap into their Latinx identities. Fostering math identities by connecting with EBs' cultural and linguistic identities can be a strong motivator. It also sends the message that you have high expectations for your EBs to succeed, just like their ancestors who made strong mathematical contributions.

## Creating a Caring Classroom Environment

In chapter 1 we discussed the importance of boosting relationships with students and parents. Similarly we need to create a caring classroom so our students will be more likely to engage in productive struggle. We want to challenge our students but at the same time care about them deeply.

Of course, part of caring means that we allow our students to persevere to solve problems because we know that is best for them. At the Japanese School, the students persevered at solving math problems because their teachers challenged them and created a friendly atmosphere of respect and caring. Nieto (2003) explains that often when teachers decide to work with students with a different cultural background than their own, they struggle to relate to the students and become frustrated and quit. In contrast, when Nieto studied the teachers that stayed on, she found that one theme common to these teachers was that they were caring.

*Create a safe atmosphere.* We want EBs to share their mathematical ideas so we can assess their thinking and develop their language proficiency. They will be more likely to share if we create a class atmosphere where they feel safe. We want math to be a "productive struggle," not just a struggle. By being caring, we can make it more productive.

*Raise social status.* It may be necessary for us to raise EBs' social status so they feel a sense of belonging. Unfortunately, some EBs are bullied because they are different. If EBs feel valued and respected by their peers, they are more likely to engage in productive struggle. We can help EBs develop social competency so that they will feel comfortable participating in meaningful mathematical discussions (Pinnow and Chval, 2014). If we value EBs, then other students will follow suit and make them feel welcome.

We want our EBs to develop mathematical arguments and critique the arguments of their peers. Thus, we need to be sure that EBs have a high social status so they can freely develop math arguments and critique their peers' arguments.

*Consider where EBs sit.* According to Pinnow and Chval (2014), positioning EBs next to students who can support them can increase their academic success in both developing language proficiency and learning math concepts. The authors maintain that if EBs are not comfortable with the students in their immediate surroundings, they have more anxiety and are less likely to open up and take risks. We can help develop EBs' math mindsets by seating them next to students who are supportive.

A preservice teacher wrote in a reflection that the EBs in the class were isolated from their peers and the non-EBs were mean to them (Ewing, 2016). She believed the EBs would improve in math if the other students in the class were kinder to them. The preservice teacher strategically placed her EBs next to students who she thought would support them.

The preservice teacher facilitated one EB to justify his answers by offering him cubes and placing him with another student with whom he worked well. The student responded positively to the preservice teacher's efforts to engage him, which suggests that when EBs sit next to supportive classmates, they will be more willing to take risks.

*Advocate for EBs.* Sometimes to create a caring classroom, we need to advocate for EBs. In a description of EBs in American schools, Valdés and Castellón (2011) maintain that the climate toward Spanish speakers—the biggest group of EBs—is unwelcoming, and that schools should be more tolerant. Teachers need to fight against these injustices and teach students that all languages and speakers of language are of equal status.

Teachers can support EBs by welcoming family members to the classroom (Lucas and Villegas, 2011). Attitudes of the other students may be more positive toward EBs if we acknowledge the value of being bilingual and bicultural. We need to advocate for our students not only so they will be more likely to solve challenging math problems but also because it is our moral obligation.

*Class community builders.* Students will also be more likely to take risks if we spend time developing the class community. As a result of being different in language proficiency and perhaps in culture, EBs will feel more comfortable in classrooms where differences are valued—creating a supportive class environment builds student confidence. While it is true that we have busy schedules, if we take the time to include community builders, such as morning meetings, students will feel happier and more productive.

*Mistakes are opportunities.* Our goal is for EBs to feel safe enough to attempt to solve challenging math problems. EBs may feel more nervous than non-EBs in rigid classrooms. After all, EBs have the challenge of expressing their mathematical arguments in a second language and will be likely to make grammar mistakes. If teachers are caring, EBs will be more likely to take risks.

Teachers can praise students who continue to persevere despite making mistakes. Teachers can also model proper behavior by admitting to the class when they make mistakes and praising students when they catch them making mistakes. There should be a class culture that shows that mistakes are opportunities to learn.

*Reduce stress to enhance working memories.* To perform well on tasks and assessments, a strong working memory is beneficial for students. Working memory not only involves remembering information but also manipulating that information. If students merely solve low-level problems, then they do not need a strong working memory, but if the goal is for students to engage in challenging, high-level problems, the working memory will need to kick in.

Thus, to engage in productive struggle, it is not enough for students to merely remember how their teacher explained a math problem in class; they also have to manipulate this information to answer the specific question being asked. However, if EBs are stressed, their working memory is affected negatively. Consequently, teachers can enhance EBs' working memories by reducing their stress.

Solving math mentally can be an effective way for EBs to develop their working memories. If teachers write the problem $99 \times 6$ on the board, the students can solve the problem by manipulating the product to $100 \times 6$ and then remembering to subtract a six from their answer. EBs will be encouraged to solve these problems if they are in a stress-free environment. Please refer to activity A.2 in appendix A for brain breaks that are culturally responsive to reduce stress.

## Questioning
Coggins (2014) explains that answering questions is a complex process for EBs—they need to focus on what the teacher is asking, develop a mathematical argument, and figure out how to use the correct words to answer the questions. Therefore when teachers ask questions, EBs are not only developing their English proficiency, they are also engaged in deep thinking. Asking probing questions can push EBs into solving rigorous problems.

*Fewer teacher explanations.* Asking questions rather than telling is an important strategy for EBs to improve their English proficiency and at the same time engage in productive struggle with math concepts. To facilitate self-discovery, we must spend less time explaining math concepts to students and more time asking them questions. Questioning is a strategy that can help students organize their thoughts and continue making sense of problems, whereas telling answers and explaining to students how to solve problems reduces the cognitive load. Please refer to activity D.2 in appendix D for a list of common math-related questions in Spanish.

*Deeper questions.* Not only should we ask a lot of questions, we should also ask questions that challenge EBs to move forward mathematically. Questions that require them to discover or justify their answers are effective—they can develop mathematical arguments with the aid of manipulatives. As the

EBs become more proficient in English, the teachers' questions should also become more complex and push EBs to justify their answers in more depth. EBs with more advanced English proficiency should be asked open questions that encourage them to answer in longer sentences.

*Assessing and advancing questions.* The purpose of assessing questions is for us to determine our students' thinking. For example, we might ask the students to explain how they got an answer. These questions not only help the teacher know what students are thinking but also develop language proficiency as they answer. After assessing students' thought processes, we can extend their thinking by asking questions that advance them—ask them if their thinking would apply to a different situation or ask them to generate a formula. Advancing questions facilitate students to engage in productive struggle. Please refer to activity D.1 in appendix D for more assessing and advancing questions for Spanish-speaking EBs.

## Time

If we want our students to persevere to solve challenging problems, we need to allow them ample time (Clark et al., 2014). EBs may need even more time than non-EBs to make sense of problems because they are doing math in another language.

One teacher didn't have time to allow students to discover how to solve problems because he had so much material to "cover" (Ewing, 2016). Eventually the teacher realized his mistake: it is short sighted to push so fast that students are left in the dust. If we do not allow EBs time to process and persevere to solve problems, they will become frustrated instead of engaging in productive struggle.

*Students, not the teacher, make sense of problems.* Instead of jumping in to explain to EBs how to solve the problems, they need time to struggle with problems on their own. All students need time to engage in productive struggle, but EBs have the extra challenge of having to translate concepts from English to Spanish and back to English. This takes time.

*Perseverance over speed.* Our goal is for students to persevere to solve problems. If we focus too much on working quickly, students will not have time to engage in productive struggle. Cathy Seeley (2015) wrote a whole book about students slowing down in math called *Faster Isn't Smarter*. Too often we reward our students who work fast instead of those who persevere. It is important for all students to be given time to persevere, but it is imperative for EBs.

*Discover over cover.* If we focus on covering the whole curriculum, EBs will not have time to do challenging tasks. Often teachers are pressured to cover large portions of content, but whenever possible we need to remind ourselves that "less is more." We might make an effort to go into great depth for at least a few topics per year. Students enjoy engaging in productive struggle, but it takes time.

## Key Ideas for Engaging in Productive Struggle

- We tend to spoon feed our students in math.
- All students, including EBs, are capable of solving challenging problems.
- We can scaffold the English, but the math should remain rigorous.
- If we have high expectations, our EBs will meet our expectations.
- EBs are more likely to engage in productive struggle if we are caring.
- We should do less telling and ask more questions.
- Solving challenging problems takes time—especially for EBs who translate from English to Spanish and back to English.
- Please refer to activity G.1 in appendix G for a self-assessment on key ideas from this chapter.

# CHAPTER FIVE

~

# Assessment

Dr. Ewing has been giving our school professional development for two years. Our scores have improved due to campus wide initiatives such as using sentence stems, and engaging students in productive struggle and student-student discourse.

—Amy, middle school math teacher from Nacogdoches ISD

This chapter on assessment is similar to chapter 2 about providing access for Spanish-speaking EBs. Indeed, we have to provide our students with access so they can complete the assessments. However, some teachers assess differently from the way they teach their day-to-day classes, making it important to dedicate a chapter to assessment.

It is hard to determine whether EBs are not performing well on mathematics assessments because we are not providing sufficient access to make them proficient with the content or because they struggle to understand the questions being asked of them. Some argue that the inadequate assessment of math knowledge is why there are disproportionately more EBs in remedial classes, lower tracks, and special education classes.

Martiniello (2009) found that language plays an important role when EBs solve mathematics problems. She studied Spanish-speaking EBs and non-EBs taking a standardized mathematics assessment given to fourth-grade students in Massachusetts. She reports that as the questions became more complex linguistically, the Spanish-speaking EBs performed worse than their peers that were at a similar level with regard to mathematics ability. She also found that the EBs performed better if Spanish-English cognates (see table 2.1—words with similar meanings such as "paralelo" and "parallel") were used.

Students do better on assessments when they can relate to the word problems. We also know that EBs perform better on word problems that have school-related vocabulary words as opposed to home-based words (Martiniello, 2009). School vocabularies are shared more equally among all students than are home-related vocabularies; home vocabularies will differ more between EBs and non-EBs. Another factor is that EBs can relate better to the test problems if they are based on school life rather than on non-EBs' home life.

We can provide EBs better access to word problems by getting to know their culture and being culturally responsive with assessment questions.

Being aware of the type of accommodations and technology that are allowed for EBs in our state for mathematics assessments is important. It may help for us to read math questions and the directions out loud to EBs until they understand what is being asked of them. Some standardized tests are translated into Spanish, so that is another option if your state permits this.

Other factors that we need to consider are using both reliable and valid assessments with EBs. Reliability is when the test is consistent over time and validity is when it measures what it is supposed to measure. For example, if a man steps on a scale and it consistently reads that he weighs 110 pounds, it is reliable, but it is not valid if he actually weighs 190 pounds (Morales, 2015).

 Most tests are not valid for EBs because they do not consider EBs' vocabulary and culture (Morales, 2015). Martiniello (2009) concluded that while assessments should use controlled vocabulary to measure EBs' aptitudes in mathematics, when not testing, teachers should develop EBs' English so they will perform better on future mathematics assessments.

It is not only good practice to meet the needs of each student, it is also the law. The Supreme Court ruled (*Lau vs. Nichols*) that treating all students the same is not fair. In other words, it is not equitable to teach EBs the same as the other students—we must teach them according to their needs. (Refer to chapter 2 for more about providing access for Spanish-speaking EBs.) Likewise, we need to select assessment questions that are culturally responsive for EBs.

The intention of No Child Left Behind was to assess all EBs' progress after one year. There were attainment targets for EBs to meet. While we don't want EBs' progress to be ignored, the attainment targets put too much pressure on teachers and EBs to perform well on standardized assessments. Presently, under the Every Student Succeeds Act, there is an attempt to reduce the pressure that teachers and EBs experience to pass assessments, but some teachers still have the mindset imposed by No Child Left Behind.

Unfortunately, the current practice of "test prep" is not effective for Spanish-speaking EBs. If teachers constantly give EBs practice for standardized assessments, they learn to dislike math. As we discussed in the first chapter, we also have to develop Spanish-speaking EBs' positive math mindsets. If we overwhelm our students with taking numerous practice tests, they will not like math and thus will actually perform worse on future standardized assessments.

In addition, if students are taking practice tests in silence, they are not developing their spoken language, which is imperative for EBs. Instead of overemphasizing the importance of taking tests and test results, we can focus on EBs' efforts. Not all students can get 100 percent on tests, but they can all give 100 percent effort.

In our high-strung test-focused classrooms, Spanish-speaking EBs can get especially anxious with assessments, so it is important to consider the following strategies to help them. The tips for assessments are grouped into the four chapters discussed so far: positive math mindsets, access, developing language, and productive struggle. The strategies are for both standardized assessments and nonstandardized tests. Accommodations for standardized assessments vary from state to state, but these tips may help teachers meet the assessment needs of Spanish-speaking EBs.

## Tips for Assessment

### Math Mindset

_Do not compare EBs with non-EBs._ Especially at the beginning stages, it is unfair to compare Spanish-speaking EBs with non-EBs. Alternatively, we need to set goals for each of our students based on their individual needs and assets.

_Avoid timed tests._ The habit of timing students during math is counterproductive. As discussed in the previous chapter, the focus of math should be for our students to persevere, not to do math quickly. Timed tests increase the stress level for each student—if students are already stressed due to linguistic and cultural challenges, timed tests will only compound the situation. Timed tests are unjust for the students who are translating math from English to Spanish and back to English.

Many students think they are bad at math because they are not as fast as their peers. We want to engage all of our students, including our Spanish-speaking EBs, but timing students makes students believe that the fast students are good at math and the slower ones are bad. We need to look for effective practices to promote each student to have a positive math identity.

*Culturally responsive.* As we discussed in chapter 1, the problems should be culturally responsive, and this applies to assessments too. There was a question on a fourth-grade state math assessment about a sub. This term has multiple meanings. The question was referring to a sandwich, but a student could think the question was about a teacher (substitute), a player (substitute), a train (subway), or a submarine.

If the designers of the assessment were familiar with cognates, they would have used the word sandwich, which is similar in Spanish. This would have been more appropriate as there were lots of Spanish-speaking students in this state required to take the assessment.

*Be supportive.* This may be obvious, but teachers have so much pressure on them that they become completely focused on test results. As a consequence, they put too much pressure on their students. Spanish-speaking EBs are taking assessments in a second language and may need even more support than other students.

*Celebrate small successes.* We want to have high expectations for EBs, but by celebrating small successes, over time we can see huge results.

*Offer choices.* All students, including Spanish-speaking EBs, like to have choices. If possible, for smaller assessments occasionally ask them what types of questions they might prefer. You may also consult with the EBs about what time to take the assessments. By giving choices—even small ones—students will be more likely to buy in and do their best. One common practice is for teachers to tell the students that they have a certain amount of time left on an activity or an assessment. Textbox 5.1 shows how teachers can tweak that comment to give students a little more choice.

The slight tweak outlined in textbox 5.1 may seem insignificant, but it is an opportunity to involve students in the decision-making process. If nobody raises their hand, the teacher can stop the activity or assessment. If some

## Textbox 5.1: Offering a Choice

- The teacher says, "Raise your hand if you need _____ more minutes."
- Students raise their hands if they need more time.
- The teacher says, "Great. You got it."

students need more time, the students are told gracefully that they have a few more minutes to finish. We need to find opportunities to give students choices and improve their positive math mindsets.

## Providing Access

*Provide visuals.* Just as it is necessary to provide access for Spanish-speaking EBs to solve class problems, we shouldn't take away these supports during assessments. Our assessments should include plenty of pictures and other visuals.

*Include graphic organizers.* Hopefully you use graphic organizers to provide access for EBs (chapter 2). Let's use them for assessments too. There is a bonus of putting Venn diagrams and concept maps on assessments—they are easy to grade. Teachers can instantly see the students' thinking with graphic organizers. Please refer to activity E.1 in appendix E for Cloze questions. These questions are similar to stem sentences and provide students access to the content being tested.

*Avoid using idioms, puns, and pronouns.* Unless the Spanish-speaking EBs are advanced and need practice, these should be avoided to provide EBs with access to the content.

*Allow dictionaries.* If permitted, we should allow EBs to use dictionaries to translate words—the assessments should be testing EBs' mathematics skills, not their English proficiency. However, some students, especially younger students, may feel overwhelmed using a dictionary and will need to be taught how to use one. It is also time consuming to use a dictionary, which is problematic because, unfortunately, many math tests are timed.

Sometimes merely translating words is still not enough for Spanish-speaking EBs. For example, if you don't know Spanish, imagine you looked up the word "quincena." Using a dictionary, you would find that this word means "fifteen." However, this translation would not help you with the cultural use of the word. In most Spanish-speaking countries, employees get paid on the fifteenth of the month, so they often say that they look forward to the "quincena."

If there were a word problem about being excited for the "quincena" to come, by merely looking up the word in the dictionary, an English speaker might miss out on the cultural meaning of the word. Likewise, EBs may struggle to answer math questions about a Mardi Gras parade if they are not used to that culture. These are examples of how culture can influence EBs on assessments and why merely allowing EBs to use dictionaries is not enough.

*Technology.* Spanish-speaking EBs tend to have less technology at home than non-EBs; they may need to be trained to use technology so it can benefit them in assessments. Teachers should make sure that EBs learn keyboarding skills and computer terms and have ample time to work on computers.

*Translate key words.* As discussed in chapter 2, we don't want to translate key words that reduce the cognitive mathematical load, but it is useful to translate key words for students so they understand what is being asked of them. We ought to translate words if necessary but avoid reducing the cognitive load by telling Spanish-speaking EBs, for example, to add when they see the word "altogether."

*Give tests in Spanish.* If your state allows this, give your EBs standardized assessments in Spanish. As far as other assessments, there are math assessments available online and most textbooks include Spanish math tests now.

*Allow EBs more time.* In chapter 4 it was discussed how Spanish-speaking EBs need ample time to engage in productive struggle. While this is true, allowing time is put under the access section because if EBs are not allowed enough time to translate and process English words, they do not have equitable access to the content. Ideally we don't time math assessments, but if we do, we need to provide extra time for students to translate from English to Spanish and back to English again.

*Read the problems to them.* If necessary, we can provide EBs with access by reading to them and discussing the problems. We should be careful not to reduce the cognitive math load, but make sure the EBs understand what the problems are asking, just as we would if it were not a test.

*Teach test-taking strategies.* Multiple-choice tests are very common in our country, but this type of assessment may be new to Spanish-speaking EBs. Instead of assuming that our EBs are incompetent if they receive a low score on a multiple-choice test, we need to teach them strategies for taking these tests.

*Alternative assessments.* As an alternative to formal tests, we can offer portfolios as a form of assessment for students. Research suggests that EBs perform better on portfolios because they do not rely so much on EBs' English proficiency (Morales, 2015). Projects also offer EBs opportunities to show what they know.

Similar to portfolios, doing projects offers Spanish-speaking EBs an alternative to more formal assessments. Topics for projects should be open because we want to give EBs choices to write about topics that are of interest to them. Having open topics also affords EBs the opportunity to draw on their home lives (Kersaint, Thompson, and Petkova, 2009). Unfortunately, teachers who do include portfolios and projects to assess EBs tend to still put more weight on the traditional written tests due to the pressure that they receive from administrators (Morales, 2015).

## Developing Language

*Zone of proximal development.* Spanish-speaking EBs benefit from developing their language throughout the day. Of course, we need to allow EBs access to the content, but the tests should be within their proximal development with regard to English complexity so that they are developing their reading and writing skills during assessments. If the assessments are too challenging linguistically, they will give up, and if they are too easy, they will not be pushed to develop their reading and writing skills.

*Assess language too.* This may be done formally or informally, but EBs spend a lot of time reading and writing during assessments. This is written evidence of their English proficiency, and we need to take note of their progress.

## Productive Struggle

*Rigorous math.* As discussed in the previous chapter, we must make the math rigorous even though we may scaffold the English. We can design assessments in such a way that Spanish-speaking EBs can excel regardless of their English proficiency.

*Be caring.* Spanish-speaking EBs may not be used to all the pressure we put on our students. Remember that they are being assessed in another language. We should spend extra time on EBs to see how they are doing emotionally so they can perform to the best of their ability.

*Reduce stress to enhance working memories.* As we mentioned in chapter 4, having a strong working memory helps students persevere to solve rigorous math problems. Unfortunately, if students are stressed, this skill is diminished.

In order to answer high-level assessment questions, it is not enough for students to merely regurgitate how their teacher explained a math problem in class; they also have to manipulate this information to answer the question being asked. Teachers can enhance EBs' working memories by reducing their stress.

*Formative assessment.* Up to now, we have discussed primarily summative assessment or formal testing, usually at the end of topics, but we should also use formative or informal assessments. Formative assessment means that we notice our students' progress and we adjust our teaching to meet their needs. One useful technique is for teachers to keep notes of formative assessments. We often do not realize how much our students improve, but when the notes are reviewed, teachers can appreciate the progress the EBs make with English proficiency and the mathematics.

*Specific feedback.* Often we are so busy that we don't find time to give our students specific feedback after assessments. By giving specific feedback, we can guide our EBs to continue trying. Furthermore, if we praise their efforts, they will be more likely to continue trying hard on each assessment.

*Self-assessments.* Whenever possible, allow opportunities to self-assess to facilitate determined, self-sufficient students.

## Key Ideas for Assessment

- EBs need access to assessment.
- If we spend too much time and pressure EBs on assessment, they will not develop their positive math mindsets.
- By providing access for our students, we can test their mathematical abilities.
- Even though we provide access, we still want to design our assessments so EBs are challenged linguistically within their zone of proximal development.
- Be caring and reduce the stress for EBs so they can engage in productive struggle.
- Please refer to activity G.1 in appendix G for a self-assessment of the key ideas on this chapter.

# CHAPTER SIX

~

# Putting It All Together

I currently work at an early learning center where children qualify to attend: Spanish as their primary language, English as a second language, economically disadvantaged, foster care, special education, or having parents in the military. For many of our children, this is their first exposure to a school setting, mathematics, and language arts. I had always heard of the "advantages of early intervention." What is amazing is witnessing it firsthand.

With math, the expectation is that the children are on the road to count to thirty at the end of one year. My bilingual teachers insist on setting the standards higher and strive for the children to count to one hundred or higher—and most of the children rise to that challenge! We have also discovered that the teaching strategies my ESL Specialist uses aren't just beneficial for students whose native language isn't English— the strategies are best practices for all of our teachers to use.

—David Rische, principal, Keller, Texas, and edutainer

David Rische points out that the strategies his teachers use for EBs are also effective for other students. Despite the fact that many of the students are receiving their first math experiences in a school setting, David's teachers have high expectations for their students. As we have discussed, if teachers have high expectations for students, they can engage in productive struggle.

One example of Spanish-speaking EBs having a positive math mindset, having access to the content, developing language, and engaging in productive struggle took place when the author of this book taught year five (fourth grade) at an international school in Spain. The class was made up mostly of students who spoke Spanish at home and learned all subjects, including math, in English. One of the most exciting times was when the class saw "Year 5 Mr. Ewi Sunny View School" on the monitor during World Math Day.

The year before, one of the students from fourth grade had come in fifty-first place in the world for this online competition. The school had an assembly for him and a big celebration, but at the end of the year Dan (pseudonym), a gifted math student, transferred to another school. There were no other students that showed his talent, but what happened after he left surpassed the Dan experience because it was a group effort.

The class discussed Dan's achievement of the previous year and together decided to enter the group competition. We were used to setting goals, so we had a choice—we could just participate in the competition, as most do, or we could try to be on the top fifty list. The students chose the latter.

We studied the previous year's results and calculated how many points we would need to be in the top fifty. Then we each set our individual goals, which if achieved would, the class thought, give us a comfortable thirty-fifth-place finish. What we did not anticipate was that world participation in the contest was to greatly increase over the previous year. Consequently, in order to be in the top fifty each student actually would have to double the score the class had planned.

One boy asked if they could have extra PE if they all got their goals. "Of course," was the answer. "If you win, you can have PE a whole day." (After all, how could a small primary school, with ten computers, one of which was broken, compete with the huge schools with computer labs from all over the world?)

The day, March 4, 2009, finally arrived. Actually the competition was for forty-eight hours because the rules were that the competition was to last as long as it was March 4 anywhere in the world. The computer lab was booked for the class at noon, which was when the competition started in Spain. What a disappointment! Most of the class couldn't even log on—the system had collapsed, and only a few managed to play before it was time for recess. The class was told that they could go to recess if they wanted or continue playing. They didn't even hear; they just played on. The entire class was staying in for recess to do math.

Finally, the students left the computer lab, and the whole school was wondering why the class had missed recess and was making so much noise. Of course, in such a short time, nobody had come close to getting their goals; they were thousands of points away from being in the top fifty. The Asian countries started earlier, and they were way ahead in the race. It was not possible to use the computer lab again for the rest of the day because other classes were engaging in the same game. The class was dismissed, and they vowed to play at home.

That evening the top fifty list was full of Australian and Korean flags. Nobody from Europe had made it because the eastern countries had an early advantage. But wait—there it was, the Spanish flag! Next to the flag was printed "Year 5, Mr. Ewi, Sunny View School" in fiftieth place. Later a British school had replaced us, but at midnight we had climbed to thirty-fourth place! That's right, students were doing math at midnight.

Oh no, in the morning it was full of American flags! While we slept, the Americans, who had a late start, rolled over everyone. Furthermore, we had no idea how many points we needed because totals were presented only for the top fifty classes. We had a big celebration in the morning, and the word was out. By that time, the whole school wanted to go to the computer lab and try their luck. It was only fair, so we stayed contained in our room, listening to the other students cheer as they had their victories. Finally we dashed up to the computer lab and tried to earn more points for our class.

Before dismissal, students were reminded that they could continue with the math game for homework, but it would be challenging to keep up with the other countries. Even if we were to get to the top fifty again, the Americans would bump us while we were sleeping, as they had the previous night. There was silence—and then someone shouted, "World Math Day, World Math Day!" Everyone gathered around him and went chanting out of the building.

That night when we went to bed we were in thirty-first place, but, as predicted, when we woke up the scoreboard was full of American flags. What could we do? We were so close. We only had three more hours before the competition closed. The Americans were sleeping, but the Asians were going full swing. Another plan was needed. Fourteen students went to the high school lab and nine more went into the primary lab. The two labs were well separated, but when "Mr. Ewi" appeared on the monitor, you could hear the shouts ring around the school.

The class answered 182,409 questions correctly and came in thirty-first place in the world! By participating in World Math Day, the students had been exposed to important life skills, such as goal setting and class community. In addition, they learned to be more open to making mistakes. In many classrooms there is a strong focus on getting the right answer, which results in students being afraid to make mistakes. By contrast, in World Math Day, students were not penalized for getting the wrong answer, so they were more open to doing the math.

## Positive Math Mindset

This reflection demonstrates how exciting it can be to work with students who have a positive math mindset. While these EBs did not skip recess often to do math, they loved the subject. Furthermore, they were confident in their abilities and were willing to take risks. The secret to facilitating these students to have a positive math mindset was to be culturally responsive, to praise effort, to make math fun, and to boost relationships.

## Providing Access

These Spanish-speaking EBs also had access to the math content. In view of the fact that the EBs spoke Spanish when outside the school environment, this was taken into account when planning math lessons. Gestures were used along with the spoken English, and speech was clear and not too fast. World Math Day itself was an example of using technology, which is multisensory and thus an effective strategy for providing access for EBs.

## Developing Language

The students were so excited about World Math Day (and doing other math projects) that they were eager to discuss and justify their mathematical arguments. Instead of doing a worksheet quietly, the students often did math in pairs and in small groups. They had plenty of opportunities to develop mathematical arguments and critique the arguments of others.

## Productive Struggle

The EBs in Spain were also a joy to teach because they engaged in productive struggle. Even though World Math Day did not promote them to engage in long tasks, they were persevering to win the game. They had learned that if they kept trying, they could be successful. Instead of spoon feeding students and trying to make math easy for them, their engagement in productive struggle was *planned*. The students learned that struggle is good and rewarding.

Because the atmosphere in the classroom was one of high expectations, the students seemed to have learned to expect more of themselves too. There was an effort to combine instruction with a caring attitude, at the same time asking many probing questions in math. Not everything about competing in World Math Day was ideal. Contrary to the principle that it is important to allow all students, including EBs, ample time to engage in productive struggle, this competition was timed, with a premium on fast responses.

Of course, the EBs in Spain are vastly different to EBs in the United States. However, this vignette is an example of how enjoyable math can be. By developing positive math mindsets, providing them access to the math, developing their language, and engaging EBs in productive struggle, math can be joyful. Despite the challenges discussed in the introduction and throughout the book that Spanish-speaking EBs may face in our schools, if we meet their needs, they will be successful. Keep flipping the pages and go to the appendices to see multiple examples of how to engage Spanish-speaking EBs in math.

## Key Ideas for Putting It All Together

- It is rewarding to work with students who have positive math mindsets.
- Activities that involve technology are multisensory and provide students with access to the math content.
- When students are excited about math, they will speak about math in depth.
- When students have high expectations about their math capabilities, there is no limit to what they can achieve.
- Please refer to activity G.1 in appendix G for a self-assessment of the key ideas in this chapter.

# Appendices

There are examples of word problems for Spanish-speaking EBs under the following categories: Positive Math Mindset (appendix A), Providing Access (appendix B), Developing Language (appendix C), Productive Struggle (appendix D), Assessment (appendix E), and Putting It All Together (appendix F). There is also a checklist (appendix G) that you can take to review your understanding of the strategies discussed in the book.

# APPENDIX A

# Positive Math Mindset

### Activity A.1: Math Plates

Be culturally responsive by tying math into students' food. Give students paper plates and let them draw food on their plate and tie it into the math

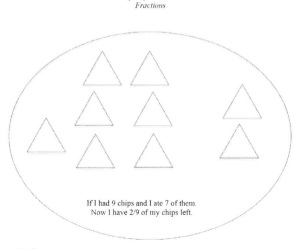

Notes: Be culturally responsive by tying math into students' food. Give students paper plates and let them draw food on their plate and tie it into the math you are doing. After drawing the food, students should include mathematical number sentences or ask a question. Displaying these plates are great visuals of mathematical concepts.

*Example of Math Plates:*
*Fractions*

If I had 9 chips and I ate 7 of them.
Now I have 2/9 of my chips left.

**Figure A.1. Math Plates**

you are doing. After drawing the food, students should include mathematical number sentences or ask a question. Displaying these plates are great visuals of mathematical concepts.

## Activity A.2: Culturally Responsive Brain Break

All students benefit from occasional brain breaks, but this is imperative for EBs because they are learning math in a second language. Let's make these brain breaks culturally responsive for the EBs. One popular game is for the leader (one student) to close his or her eyes and count to ten out loud. Meanwhile the other students move quietly to one of four corners. The leader randomly calls out a number from one to four. The students in the corner that is called have to sit down. The leader counts to ten again and the remaining students hide in another corner. This game is played until only one or a few students remain.

The game in activity A.2 can be adapted to celebrate different countries or cities. The numbers one to four can be changed to countries that the students are from. For example, the students would hide in Mexico, Honduras, El Salvador, or Cuba. A variation would be to hide in corners "uno, dos, tres, or cuatro." A third variation would be to change the four corners to mathematical terms in Spanish. For example, hide in "círculo, cuadrado, tríangulo, or rectángulo." These variations would be just as fun for the whole class and make the EBs feel valued.

# APPENDIX B

~

# Providing Access

## Activity B.1: Sentence Stems—Shapes

The strength of this exercise is that students have access to the content and can learn about shapes in depth. Textbooks typically only offer one or two examples of shapes and that causes misconceptions. Often students think that if you turn a triangle, it is no longer a triangle because in most of the examples shown in textbooks, the bases of the triangles are parallel to the bottom page.

This exercise offers students a definition of shapes, examples, nonexamples, and a built-in assessment with pictures. Students can write in Spanish or in both English and Spanish. In the first part of activity B.1, the blanks can be filled in for any shape, and in the second part of activity B.1 the blanks are filled in for a parallelogram.

### *Activity B.1: An Example of Sentence Stems—Shapes*

A parallelogram is a shape with two sets of parallel sides.
Un paralelogramo es una forma con dos pares de lados paralelos.

These are parallelograms.
Estos son paralelogramos.

These are NOT parallelograms.
Estos NO son paralelogramos.

Are these parallelograms?
¿Son estos paralelogramos?

Figure B.1.   An Example of Sentence Stems—Shapes

## Activity B.2: Graphic Organizer Alphabet

This visual approach allows teachers to display math terms being used in alphabetical order. After explaining a term, teachers can write the definition and include drawings on a sticky note or index card. These notes can be put under the appropriate letter to help students organize their thoughts.

| A | B | C | D | E | F | G | H | I |
|---|---|---|---|---|---|---|---|---|
| J | K | L | M | N | O | P | Q | R |
| S | T | U | V | W | X | Y | Z | |

**Figure B.2.**

APPENDIX C

# Developing Language

## Activity C.1: Reciprocal Teaching

Reciprocal teaching is popular in reading and it is effective because the students assume the role of teachers. Each student is assigned a role: predictor, clarifier, or summarizer. There are typically four steps in reciprocal teaching for reading, but groups of three are often more effective for group work so the questioner role is taken out—all three students ask questions.

In Spanish there are no words for "do" and "did" so having practice to ask questions is an important skill. At the beginning stages, EBs will have interference from Spanish and say sentences like, "We have recess now?" They tend to leave out "Do" because it is not used in Spanish.

**Table C.1.  Student Roles in Reciprocal Teaching of Reading**

| Name of Role | Description of Role |
| --- | --- |
| Predictor | The predictor decides who will read the problem out loud. With the help of the group, the predictor guesses what the problem is asking. |
| Clarifier | With the help of the group, the clarifier asks questions to advance the group's thinking. For example, he or she might ask the group what the next step is. |
| Summarizer | With the help of the group, the summarizer reviews the important steps solved. This review should be done throughout the lesson and at the end. The summarizer can also discuss how he or she can solve the problem more efficiently the next time. |

**Table C.2  An Example of Reciprocal Teaching**

This is an example of how students might solve the following problem using reciprocal teaching:

Mariana had so much fun at her sister's quinceañera celebration this weekend. The mass was exciting, but Mariana especially liked the waltz afterward. She danced for hours. When she finally stopped dancing, she looked around and counted 275 people at the celebration. How much was it going to cost to feed all of those people? If 35 people did not eat and everyone else had one plate, how many people ate? How much did the food cost if each plate cost $7.99?

| Role | Possible Questions | Possible Answers |
|---|---|---|
| Predictor | 1. Who would like to read the problem? | 1. One of the group members volunteers to read. |
| Clarifier | 2. What are the key vocabulary words in this problem? | 2. A "quinceañera" is a party given to girls who turn fifteen. |
| | 3. What does "mass" mean in this problem? | 3. Mass is referring to a church service, not weight. |
| Predictor | 4. What is the question asking? | 4. How much does the food cost altogether? |
| | 5. What operation or operations might we use? | 5. It looks like we all need to multiply because one plate costs $7.99. So how much would all the plates cost? |
| | 6. What might be a sensible answer be? | 6. Because there are a lot of people at the quinceañera party, there will be a big number. |
| Summarizer | 7. What have we learned so far? | 7. We are calculating how much the food costs altogether at a quinceañera party. We may multiply. |
| Clarifier | 8. What are the steps needed to solve this problem? | 8. We know there are 275 people at the celebration, but we need to calculate how many people ate a plate of food. |
| | 9. How can we decide how many people ate food? | 9. There are 275 and all but 35 had food so we can subtract 35 from 275. |
| | 10. How many ate food? | 10. 275 minus 35 is 240. 240 people. |

| Role | | |
|---|---|---|
| Summarizer | 11. What have we solved so far? | 11. 275 minus 35 gives us the total of how many people ate. 240 people ate a plate of food. |
| Clarifier | 12. Great. We are getting there. What is the next step? | 12. We need to find out how much was spent on food altogether. |
| | 13. How can we get the answer? | 13. We know that 240 people had food and each plate costs $7.99. We can multiply to get the answer. |
| Summarizer | 14. Let's review. Why do we multiply? | 14. We multiply because one person pays $7.99 for a plate, so if 240 had food, we would multiply. |
| Clarifier | 15. Let's multiply 240 by $7.99. | 15. The answer is $1,917.60. |
| | 16. Does the answer make sense? | 16. It is a lot of money, but there are also a lot of people there. So yes, it makes sense. |
| Summarizer | 17. What did we learn? | 17. We learned that it costs a lot of money to feed so many people. |
| | 18. Did everyone participate in the problem? Can each of us explain how we got the answer? | 18. The group answers if each member participated and can explain the problem. |

## Activity C.2: Math Games

The purpose of the following games is to develop students' math concepts and language. If they do a worksheet quietly at their desk, they do not talk or listen. With these games, they will have the added benefit of promoting math mindsets because they can be fun. All of the games are designed to be played in pairs. These games can be tweaked to meet your students' grade level and interest.

Teachers find it useful for students to play games when they finish their work. However, some students take longer to do their work and never or rarely get to play the games. If students have to translate from English to Spanish to English, they may learn to hate math if they don't have opportunities to play the games. Thus, be equitable and allow all students to play.

### I Spy a Shape

Students play I Spy with a shape in the room. Sentence stems can be made to facilitate students' access. For example, I spy with my eye, a shape that is _____ (color) and close to the _____ (object). When using colors consider that about 8 percent of males are colorblind. Teachers can also hang shapes around the room to make the game more fun.

### Cultural Coin Toss

There are lots of coin tossing games. Instead of using American currency, you can use coins from other countries. Students may volunteer to bring coins in for the day. Most students like to predict if a coin toss is heads or tails (cara or cruz). They can guess how many times the coin will be tails if tossed thirty times. If two coins are flipped, students can guess how many times both coins will be tails.

### How Many "Mazapanes" (Latin Candy) in the Jar?

Instead of asking students to guess how many candies are in the jar, you can put in some food that your Spanish-speaking EBs like. Typically the teacher fills the jar and all the students write down their guess. By working in pairs, students can discuss their thinking and have to come to a consensus for their guess. Marzipans are very popular in many Latin countries, especially around Christmastime. An alternative could be for students to use math strategies to calculate how many "frijoles" would fill up a jar or classroom.

First to 30

The object of this game is for a student to say the number "30." Students count from 1 to 30, but the game gets harder because each student says one, two, or three consecutive numbers. For example, the first player might say "1" and the second player might say "2, 3, 4." The winner is the student that gets to say "30." Students can play in Spanish. The range of numbers can be changed, for example from 1 through 5, to meet the students' level of logic. For practice in addition, instead of counting, the students can say they are going to add one, two, or three to the running total.

# Productive Struggle

### Activity D.1: Assessing and Advancing Questions

Following is a problem about Veronica's Christmas Rosca or cake. The teacher asks assessing questions and then pushes the student deeper into the problem with a few advancing questions. The student's English in this example is advanced. If the EB were at an earlier English proficiency level, she could perhaps still make the same mathematical argument but would need more access to the problem and might use drawings or Spanish to justify her answers.

*It is Christmastime and Veronica is excited. Now that she lives in the United States she celebrates Christmas and Santa Claus, but her favorite part of the holiday is still on January 6 (El Día de los Reyes). She loves eating Rosca de Reyes. The cake is delicious, but the best part is guessing who will get the hidden baby in their slice.*

*Last year her uncle and mom got the plastic baby in their cake. Everyone says that whoever gets the baby has to host a party on February 2, Día de la Candelaria—Veronica doesn't think they will make her host a party, but will her slice of cake have the baby? What is the probability that the plastic baby will be in your slice of cake?*

**Table D.1.**

| Teacher's Question | Type of Question | Student's Answer | Notes |
|---|---|---|---|
| Do you like Rosca? | Affective | Yes. I like it. | Teachers should allow students time to make sense of the math on their own before asking questions. |
| What is the question asking? | Assessing | If I will get the baby. | The teacher wants to know if the student understands the probability of the question so she continues to assess. |
| Tell me more. | Assessing | The question asks what the probability is that I get the baby. | Probability is a cognate: la probabalidad. |
| How do you say probability in Spanish? | Assessing | La probabilidad | The teacher shows appreciation for Spanish and assesses the student's understanding of vocabulary. |
| How can we calculate the probability or la probabilidad? | Assessing | We need to know how many slices there are in the Rosca. | This problem is open on purpose. The student recognizes that more information is needed. |
| Okay. Do you have Rosca on Reyes? | Affective | Yes! | The teacher does not assume that all Latinx have Rosca. |
| Let's use your family's example. How many people might have a piece of Rosca? | Assessing | It depends, but we usually share with our neighbors. Maybe ten. | Now the math is personal to the student. |
| What is the probability that you get the plastic baby in your slice of cake? | Assessing | If there are ten slices and I have one slice, then the probability is one out of ten that it is in my slice. | The teacher realizes that the student has a basic understanding of the problem and now wants to advance her thinking. |
| Is there anyone in your family that doesn't like Rosca much? | Advancing | My brother doesn't like it very much. He often has a small piece. | The student is ready to delve deeper into the problem now. |

| | | | |
|---|---|---|---|
| Hmmm. | Advancing | Ahh so if his piece is smaller the probability changes. | The teacher did not need to ask a question. The student's wheels are spinning. |
| Work more on this problem and I will be back in a few minutes to check on you. | Advancing | Okay. | The teacher is leaving the problem open so the student can solve it how she wants. |
| After ten minutes the teacher asks how the student is doing. | Assessing | Wow. This is so interesting. I realized that my brother often has a smaller piece and my sister loves Rosca so she has a bigger piece than the rest of us. It is not exact but if there are ten slices, we all will have a one in ten chance of getting the baby except for my brother and sister. If his piece is half as big as the other pieces then the probability that he gets the baby is one out of twenty. If my sister eats his other piece, the probability for her is three out of twenty. | The student has realized an important concept about probability. If the size of the cake increases, so does the probability. Each person will only have the same probability of having the baby if they have the same size cake. |
| What did you learn? | Assessing | That the probability depends on the size of cake. | It is effective to ask students to summarize their thinking. |
| Would this problem work with other problems? | Advancing | I think so. | The student is ready to generalize the problem. |
| Please come up with a similar problem about probability and be ready to share it with me or a friend. | Advancing | Okay. I will think of another problem. | The student is challenged because the math is relevant to her life and she is engaged in productive struggle. |

## Activity D.2: Common Questions in Spanish Useful in Math Class

The questions are purposefully short and to the point so the teacher who does not speak Spanish fluently can ask questions to engage her EBs.

**Table D.2.**

| English | Spanish |
| --- | --- |
| What is the question? | ¿Cúal es la pregunta? |
| Explain your thinking. | Explícate. |
| Why? | ¿Por qúe? |
| Do you agree? | ¿De acuerdo? |
| Does everyone agree? | ¿Todos estan de acuerdo? |
| Are you sure? | ¿Seguro? |
| True? | ¿Verdad? |
| Always true? | ¿Verdad siempre? |
| And now? (What's next?) | ¿Y ahora? |
| What is the rule? | ¿Cúal es la regla? |
| Does it make sense? | ¿Tiene sentido? |
| How do you know? | ¿Cómo lo sabes? |
| Can you do it another way? | ¿Puedes hacerlo de otra manera? |
| Do you want to share? | ¿Quieres compartir? |
| What did you learn? | ¿Qúe aprendiste? |

# APPENDIX E

# Assessment

## Activity E.1: Cloze Test Questions

Cloze exercises are similar to sentence stems mentioned in chapter 2. Cloze questions can provide EBs access to the content because they don't have to write a lot. Another advantage is that the questions are open and students can put in different answers depending on their mathematical and English proficiency levels. Notice the questions are short and in the present tense to provide access.

1. Manuel's favorite soccer player is Leonardo Messi. He is from Argentina and plays for Barcelona. Messi scores _____ goals. How many more goals will he need to score to have a total of _____ goals?

2. Juan wants to make arroz con leche. He buys rice, milk, cinnamon, and sugar. Normally Juan needs half a cup of rice, one cinnamon stick, three cups of milk, and a third of a cup of sugar. If Juan wants to make the recipe _____ times as big, he will need _____ cup/s of rice, _____ cinnamon stick/s, _____ cups of milk, and _____ cup/s of sugar.

3. It is Nora's birthday and she has a piñata. There are _____ dulces (sweets) in the piñata. There are _____ people at the birthday party. How many dulces do they need to have in the piñata so each person has _____ dulces?

4. Maria scores _____ out of _____ penalty kicks. How many consecutive penalty kicks will she need to score to be successful _____ percent of the time?

# Putting It All Together

## Activity F.1: Beginning, Middle, and End of Math Lessons

**Table F.1.   Teacher Actions and Resulting Benefits**

| Beginning or Before Math Lessons | |
|---|---|
| *Teacher Action* | *Benefit* |
| Greet students at the door. | This boosts relationships and reduces stress. If students feel safe, they will take risks to solve math problems and engage in **productive struggle**. |
| Ask students to stand up and when they hear the music, find a temporary partner to share with. | Moving around the room gets the brain ready to learn. Students' stress is reduced as the class community is developed and facilitates students engaging in **productive struggle**. Music can put students in a positive state to learn math, which develops students' **positive math mindsets**. |
| Students share what they know about a concept or what they remember from a previous lesson. | Students **develop their language** as they have opportunities to share with a classmate. Teachers can learn students' background knowledge and adjust the lesson accordingly. |
| Students give their partners a high five and return to their seats. | After having a positive interaction with a classmate, students are ready to have a positive interaction with math problems and engage in **productive struggle**. |

| *Middle or During Math Lessons* | |
|---|---|
| *Teacher Action* | *Benefit* |
| Briefly introduce the problems. Use visuals. | Students are ready to solve the problems after talking with a partner. Using visuals **provides them access**. |
| Relate the problems to the students' lives. | Students will like math more if it is related to their lives. Being culturally responsive can develop students' **positive math mindsets**. |
| Allow students time to make sense of the problems themselves. | It takes time for students to engage in **productive struggle**. |
| Ask assessing and advancing questions. | By asking students questions such as, "How did you solve that problem?" you know what to do next. If the students have solved the problem efficiently, you can ask an advancing question, which pushes them to delve deeper into the content. Asking advancing questions **develops language** and engages students in **productive struggle**. |
| Take a short brain break every twenty to twenty-five minutes. | All students benefit from breaks, but breaks are imperative for students learning math in a second language. Taking breaks can develop **positive math mindsets**. |

| *End or Closing Math Lessons* | |
|---|---|
| *Teacher Action* | *Benefit* |
| Toward the end of the lesson, encourage students to write what they have learned. | By allowing students opportunities to write, we **develop their language**. Furthermore, the process of thinking and writing about what they have learned cements learning and increases retention. |
| Have students share what they have learned with a partner. | Sharing with a partner develops class community (**productive struggle**), increases retention, and **develops students' language**. Furthermore, students can increase their knowledge of math facts as they discuss concepts. |
| Thank students for persevering. | If we want our students to persevere and engage in **productive struggle**, we should reward that behavior when it occurs. |

## Activity F.2: Evaluating Lesson Plans

### Positive Math Mindsets

- Is my lesson plan culturally responsive for my EBs?
- Will I focus on students' efforts?
- Is the lesson fun and related to my Spanish-speaking students' lives?
- Do I provide opportunities in the lesson to boost my relationship with the EBs?

### Providing Access

- Do each of my EBs have access to this lesson?
- Did I plan this lesson with my EBs in mind or was it written for non-EBs?
- Do I include sentence stems?
- Do I include graphic organizers?

### Developing Language

- Will my EBs have opportunities to speak with partners or in small groups?
- Have I structured the lesson to engage my students to read and write in this lesson?

### Productive Struggle

- Will this lesson be mathematically challenging for the EBs?
- Do the students have ample time to engage in productive struggle?

# APPENDIX G

# Checklists

## Activity G.1: Checklist

Please reflect on the following key ideas to help determine where you currently stand at meeting the needs of Spanish-speaking EBs in math. After reflecting on these "I can . . ." statements, analyze in which areas you would like to improve and set a goal so you can better meet the needs of your students.

### *Key Ideas for Developing Positive Math Mindsets*

- I can facilitate each student in my class to have a positive math mindset—a belief that they can do math if they work hard, are passionate about math, and are willing to take risks.
- I can facilitate each of my EBs to have a positive math mindset.
- I can relate the math to my EBs by being culturally responsive.
- I can appreciate my EBs' efforts to learn both math and English at the same time.
- I can make math fun instead of drilling and encourage EBs to be passionate about math.
- I can boost the relationship with my Spanish-speaking EBs so they will be more likely to take risks in math and enjoy it.

## *Key Ideas for Providing Access*

- I can learn some of my EBs' algorithms and symbols for learning math.
- I can provide my EBs access to math.
- I can take into consideration the needs of my EBs at the time of planning rather than trying to adapt them after the lessons are already made.
- I can meet with my EBs before the math lesson to preteach vocabulary words and background knowledge.
- I can speak to my EBs using GRASSES (gestures; repeat; avoid idioms, pronouns, and jokes; speak slowly; simple sentences; be expressive; and smile).
- I can use scaffolding techniques to provide EBs access to solve the math content.

## *Key Ideas for Developing Language*

- I can develop my EBs' language in all classes, including math class, so they can solve math problems on their own.
- I can develop language by giving EBs ample opportunities to listen, speak, read, and write.
- I can teach tier 2 words as well as technical math words to EBs.
- I can respect the EBs if they go through a silent period.
- I can help EBs feel safe and accepted so they are more likely to take the chance to share their ideas.
- I can consider EBs' level of English proficiency when I ask them questions. At the beginning stages I can ask yes/no questions, but later I can push them by asking open questions that require longer answers.
- I can offer EBs many opportunities to reading and write in math class.

## *Key Ideas for Engaging in Productive Struggle*

- I can refrain from spoon feeding EBs in math.
- I can engage EBs to solve challenging problems.
- I can scaffold the English but keep the math rigorous for EBs.
- I can have high expectations for EBs so they meet my expectations.
- I can be caring with my EBs so they will be more likely to engage in productive struggle.
- I can do less telling and ask more questions.
- I can provide my EBs time to solve challenging problems.

## Key Ideas for Assessment

- I can provide my EBs access to assessment.
- I can reduce the pressure I put on EBs so they will develop positive math mindsets.
- I can provide access for EBs so I can test their mathematical abilities.
- I can provide access and design my assessments so EBs are challenged linguistically within their zone of proximal development.
- I can be caring and reduce the stress for EBs so they can engage in productive struggle.

## Key Ideas for Putting It All Together

- I can facilitate my EBs to have positive math mindsets so they are passionate about math, believe they can do math if they work hard, and are willing to take risks to solve math problems.
- I can let my EBs use technology to have access to the content.
- I can help my EBs be passionate about math so they are eager to explain and justify concepts.
- I can have high expectations for EBs so they will persevere and engage in productive struggle.
- I can develop my EBs' positive math mindsets, provide them access to the content, develop their language, and engage them in productive struggle.
- I can apply the strategies discussed in this book so my EBs can be successful in math.

~

# References

Abedi, J., and Lord, C. (2001). The language factor in mathematics tests. *Applied Measurement in Education, 14*(3), 219–34.

August, D. E., and Shanahan, T. (2006). *Developing literacy in second-language learners: Report of the National Literacy Panel on Language-Minority Children and Youth.* Mahwah, NJ: Lawrence Erlbaum Associates.

Boaler, J. (2015). *Mathematical mindsets: Unleashing students' potential through creative math, inspiring messages and innovative teaching.* Hoboken, NJ: John Wiley and Sons.

Borgioli, G. M. (2008). Equity for English language learners in mathematics classrooms. *Teaching Children Mathematics, 15*(3), 185–91.

Bresser, R., Melanese, K., and Sphar, C. (2009). *Supporting English language learners in math class: Grades 3–5.* Sausalito, CA: Math Solutions Publications.

Celedon-Pattichis, S., and Ramirez, R. (2012). Beyond setting high expectations. In S. Celedon-Pattichis and N. Ramirez (Eds.), *Beyond good teaching: Advancing mathematics education for EBs,* 1–30. Reston, VA: National Council of Teachers of Mathematics.

Clarke, D., Roche, A., Sullivan, P., and Cheeseman, J. (2014). Creating a classroom culture that encourages students to persist on cognitively demanding tasks. In K. S. Karp and National Council of Teachers of Mathematics (Eds.), *Using research to improve instruction* (pp. 67–76). Reston, VA: National Council of Teachers of Mathematics.

Coggins, D. (2014). *English language learners in the mathematics classroom.* Thousand Oaks, CA: Corwin Press.

Cummins, J. (1981). Four misconceptions about language proficiency in bilingual education. *NABE Journal, 5*(3), 31–45.

de Jong, E. J., and Harper, C. A. (2011). "Accommodating diversity": Pre-service teachers' views on effective practices for English language learners. In T. Lucas (Ed.), *Teacher preparation for linguistically diverse classrooms: A resource for teacher educators* (pp. 73–90). New York: Routledge.

Dixon, J. K., Adams, T. L., and Nolan, E. C. (2015). *Beyond the common core: A handbook for mathematics in a PLC at work.* Bloomington, IN: Solution Tree Press.

Dweck, C. S. (2007). *Mindset: The new psychology of success.* New York: Random House.

Dweck, C. (2015). Carol Dweck revisits the growth mindset. *Education Week, 35*(5), 20–24.

Ebe, A. (2010). Culturally relevant texts and reading assessment for English language learners. *Reading Horizons, 50*(3), 193–210.

EDFacts. 2015. *State assessments in reading/language arts and mathematics: School year 2014–2015 EDFacts Data Documentation.* Washington, DC: U.S. Department of Education.

Ewing, J. (2016). Pre-service elementary teachers learning to facilitate students' engagement of the common core state standards' mathematical practices: Balancing attention to English language learners, to all learners, and to one's own mathematical learning. Unpublished doctoral dissertation, Syracuse, New York.

Ewing, J. (2017). Preparing pre-service teachers to teach ELLs in methods courses. *Journal of Mathematics Teacher Education in Texas, 7*(3), 3–4.

Ewing, J. (2018). Considering ELLs when planning lessons. *Ohio Journal of School Mathematics, 78*(1), 52–56.

Ewing, J., Gresham, G., and Dickey, B. (2019). Pre-service teachers learning to engage all students, including English language learners, in productive struggle. *Issues in the Undergraduate Mathematics Preparation of School Teachers: The Journal, 2*, 52–56.

Feitelson, D., and Goldstein, Z. (1986). Patterns of book ownership and reading to young children in Israeli school-oriented and nonschool oriented families. *The Reading Teacher, 39*, 224–30.

Ferlazzo, L., and Sypnieski, K. H. (2018). *The ELL teacher's toolbox: Hundreds of practical ideas to support your students.* Hoboken, NJ: John Wiley and Sons.

Frey, N., Hattie, J., and Fisher, D. (2018). *Developing assessment-capable visible learners, grades K–12: Maximizing skill, will, and thrill.* Thousand Oaks, CA: Corwin Press.

Gándara, P., Rumberger, R., Maxwell-Jolly, J., and Callahan, R. (2003). English learners in California schools: Unequal resources, unequal outcomes. *Education Policy Analysis Archives, 11*(36), 1–54.

Garrison, L., Ponce, G., and Amaral, O. (2007). Ninety percent of the game is half mental. *Teaching Children Mathematics, 14*, 12–17.

Gorski, P. C. (2018). *Reaching and teaching students in poverty: Strategies for erasing the opportunity gap.* New York: Teachers College Press.

Hattie, J. (2009). *Visible learning: A synthesis of over 800 meta-analyses relating to achievement.* New York: Routledge.

Hiebert, J., and Grouws, D. A. (2007). The effects of classroom mathematics teaching on students' learning. In F. K. Lester Jr. (Ed.), *Second handbook of research on mathematics teaching and learning* (pp. 371–404). Charlotte, NC: Information Age Publishing.

Howard, G. R. (2006). *We can't teach what we don't know: White teachers, multiracial schools.* New York: Teachers College Press.

Hufford-Ackles, K., Fuson, K., and Sherin, M. (2004). Describing levels and components of a math-talk learning community. *Journal for Research in Mathematics Education, 35*(2), 81.

Jensen, E. (2013). *Engaging students with poverty in mind: Practical strategies for raising achievement.* Alexandria, VA: ASCD.

Jensen, E. (2019). *Poor students, rich teaching: Seven high-impact mindsets for students from poverty (using mindsets in the classroom to overcome student poverty and adversity).* Bloomington, IN: Solution Tree.

Kersaint, G., Thompson, D. R., and Petkova, M. (2009). *Teaching mathematics to English language learners.* New York: Routledge.

Kilpatrick, J., Swafford, J., and Findell, B. (2001). *Adding it up: Helping children learn mathematics.* Washington, DC: National Academy Press.

Koestler, C., Felton, M. D., Bieda, K., and Otten, S. (2013). *Connecting the NCTM Process Standards and the Common Core State Standards for mathematics practices to improve instruction.* Reston, VA: National Council of Teachers of Mathematics.

Krashen, S., and Brown, C. L. (2005). The ameliorating effects of high socioeconomic status: A secondary analysis. *Bilingual Research Journal, 29*(1), 185–96.

Ladson-Billings, G. (2009). *The dreamkeepers: Successful teachers of African American children.* Second edition. Hoboken, NJ: John Wiley and Sons.

Larson, M. R., Fennell, F., Adams, T., Dixon, J., Kobett, B., and Wray, J. (2012). *Common Core mathematics in a PLC at work.* Bloomington, IN: Solution Tree Press.

Lucas, T. (2011). Language, schooling, and the preparation of teachers for linguistic diversity. In T. Lucas (Ed.), *Teacher preparation for linguistically diverse classrooms: A resource for teacher educators* (pp. 3–17). New York: Routledge.

Lucas, T., and Villegas, A. M. (2011). A framework for preparing linguistically responsive teachers. In T. Lucas (Ed.), *Teacher preparation for linguistically diverse classrooms: A resource for teacher educators* (pp. 55–72). New York: Routledge.

Maldonado, L., Turner, E., Dominguez, H., and Empson, S. (2009). English language learners learning from and contributing to mathematical discussion. In D. White and J. Spitzer (Eds.), *Mathematics for every student: Responding to diversity, grades PreK–5* (pp. 7–22). Reston, VA: National Council of Teachers of Mathematics.

Martiniello, M. (2009). Linguistic complexity, schematic representations, and differential item functioning for English language learners in math tests. *Educational Assessment, 14*(3), 160–79.

Meyer, A., Rose, D. H., and Gordon, D. (2014). *Universal design for learning: Theory and practice*. Wakefield, MA: CAST Professional Publishing.

Milner IV, H. R. (2015). *Rac(e)ing to class: Confronting poverty and race in schools and classrooms*. Cambridge, MA: Harvard Education Press.

Morales, P. (2015). Content review and practice book for the Texas Educator Certification Program: 154 English as second language supplemental. ELLservices.org.

Moschkovich, J. (2007). Examining mathematical discourse practices. *For the Learning of Mathematics, 27*, 24–30.

Murrey, D. L. (2008). Differentiating instruction in mathematics for the English language learner. *Mathematics Teaching in the Middle School, 14*(3), 146–53.

National Council of Teachers of Mathematics. (2014). *Principles to action: Ensuring mathematical success for all*. Reston, VA: National Council of Teachers of Mathematics.

Nieto, S. (2003). *Identity and language learning: Gender, ethnicity and educational change*. New York: Teachers College Press.

Pinnow, R., and Chval, B. (2014). Positioning ELLs to develop academic, communicative, and social competencies in mathematics. In M. Civil and E. Turner (Eds.), *Common Core State Standards in mathematics for English language learners* (pp. 21–34). Alexandria, VA: Teachers of English to Speakers of Other Languages, Inc.

Seeley, C. L. (2015). *Faster isn't smarter: Messages about math, teaching, and learning in the 21st century: A resource for teachers, leaders, policy makers, and families*. Sausalito, CA.

Silver, D., Saunders, M., and Zarate, E. (2008). What factors predict high school graduation in the Los Angeles Unified School District? Santa Barbara: California Dropout Research Project.

Turner, E., Celedón-Pattichis, S., Marshall, M., and Tennison, A. (2009). "Fíjense amorcitos, les voy a contar una historia": The power of story to support solving and discussing mathematical problems with Latino/a kindergarten students. In *Mathematics for every student: Responding to diversity, grades Pre-K–5*, (pp. 23–41). Reston, VA: National Council of Teachers of Mathematics.

Turner, E. E., Drake, C., McDuffie, A. R., Aguirre, J., Bartell, T. G., and Foote, M. Q. (2012). Promoting equity in mathematics teacher preparation: A framework for advancing teacher learning of children's multiple mathematics knowledge bases. *Journal of Mathematics Teacher Education, 15*, 67–82.

Valdés, G., and Castellón, M. (2011). English language learners in American schools: Characteristics and challenges. In T. Lucas (Ed.), *Teacher preparation for linguistically diverse classrooms: A resource for teacher educators* (pp. 127–42). New York: Routledge.

Verdugo, R. R., and Flores, B. (2007). English-language learners: Key issues. *Education and Urban Society, 39*(2), 167–93.

Vygotsky, L. S. (1978). *Mind in society: The development of higher psychological processes*. Cambridge, MA: Harvard University.

Zahner, W. (2012). Discussing conceptually demanding mathematics in a bilingual algebra class. In S. Celedón-Pattichis and N. G. Ramirez (Eds.), *Beyond good teaching: Advancing mathematics education for EBs* (pp. 103–8). Reston, VA: National Council of Teachers of Mathematics.

Zwiers, J. (2008). *Building academic language: Essential practices for content classrooms, grades 5–12.* San Francisco: Jossey-Bass.

# Index

visual(s):
    brain break, 21, 64, 88
    cultural and linguistic needs, 32–36
    math projects and fairs, 21
    pictures, photos, and acting, 43–45,
    49, 53–55, 61, 75, 91, 107
vocabulary:
    culturally responsive, 29
    linguistic barriers, 28

    mathematical language, 17, 34, 46, 47
    pre-teach, 32, 44, 56
    speaking and listening, 48, 49, 53–56
    writing, sketching, 57, 58

working memories, 68, 77
workshops, teachers, 63 , 71, 121
World Math Day, 80–82

~

# About the Author

Dr. **Jim Ewing** was born in Ithaca, New York, and now lives in Texas, where he is an assistant professor at Stephen F. Austin State University. His teaching, research, and service focus on teaching math to Spanish-speaking English language learners (ELLs) preferably identified as emergent bilinguals (EBs). He has published seven articles about math and EBs. He was an elementary teacher in both the United States and Spain for twenty-five years and an administrator for eight years at an international school in Spain.

Jim is trained by Eric Jensen to give motivating workshops to teachers about how to teach math to each student. Not only do you learn strategies but also you empathize with EBs when Jim teaches a math lesson in Spanish. To learn more about his workshops and to read current articles, go to EwingLearning.com.